BLACKWATER

BLACKWATER

PAULETTE JILES

ALFRED A. KNOPF

NEW YORK 1988

THIS IS A BORZOI BOOK
PUBLISHED BY ALFRED A. KNOPF, INC.

Certain of the poems in this volume were originally published, in some instances in somewhat different form, in the author's books Waterloo Express (1973) and Celestial Navigation (1984), and are reprinted by permission of their publishers, House of Anansi Press and McClelland & Stewart, respectively. A somewhat different version of A Manual of Etiquette for Ladies Crossing Canada by Train was originally published by Polestar Press, in 1987, this under the title Sitting in the Club Car Drinking Rum and Karma-Kola. The short story "Dune Trek," two letters, certain poems, certain prose pieces, and The James Poems were first published in The Quarterly. The author is grateful to the foregoing publishers for their courtesy in permitting her to reprint such work herein.

Library of Congress Cataloging-in-Publication Data
Jiles, Paulette [date]
Blackwater.
I. Title.
PR9199.3.J54B55   1988   811'.54   87–46103
ISBN 0–394–56862–1

Manufactured in the United States of America

FIRST EDITION

To my aunts
Maxie, Mayme, Donna, Jenny Noon, and Byatt, with love

I wish to convey deepest thanks to Gordon Lish for his splendid and generous encouragement, and for his incisive editing of many different pieces of varying approaches and styles, which made this collection possible; and to Liz Darhansoff, and to Caroline, Jeff, Joanie, the Elizabeths, Pauline, Fred, Robert B., and the writers' community of Nelson, British Columbia.

P.J.

ᓂᐢᑕᒼ ᐁᐸᑭᑕᓇᒧᔭᐣ ᐱᒪᑎᓯᐧᐃᐣ ᓂᒪᒪᑲᒃ ᐁᑭ
ᐅᒋ ᐱᒪᑎᓯᔭᐣ ᐁᐧᑲ ᒧᔕᒃ ᓂᑲ ᑌᐱᓇᐧᐁᐢᓯᐣᑕ
ᐧᐊ ᓂᒪᒪ ᒥᓇ ᓂᐱᒪᒋᐃᐧᐁᒼ᙮

ᒥᓇ ᓂᑭ ᑭᑭᓄᐦᐊᒪᒃ ᒪᒋᑫᑯᓇᐠ ᐅᒋ ᒥᓇ ᑫᑯᓇᐣ
ᑲᒥᐧᓇᔑᑭᐣ ᐁᑭ ᑭᑭᓄᐦᐊᒪᐧᐃᔑ- ᐁᑲ ᒋᒪᓀᐣᒋ
ᑫᐧᐊᒃ ᒥᓇ ᐁᑭ ᑭᑭᓄᐦᐊᒪᐧᐃᔑ- ᐁᔑᓇᐧᑲᒃ ᐅ
ᐧᐁ ᐱᒪᑎᓯᐧᐃᐣ ᒣᐧᑲ- ᑲᐱᒪᒋᓯᐣᑕᒪᒃ᙮

First of all, when I took my first breath of life, my mother made it possible for me to have a life, and for that I am grateful to the Creator. She would teach me right from wrong, and always told me neither to get into trouble nor stir it up. She taught me the facts of life, all of which I am going through now.

—AGNES WENJACK, of Ogoki Post;
her winning entry in *The Wawatay News*
"I Have the Best Mother in the North" contest.

CONTENTS

BLACKWATER

The first one was a charm against nakedness;
everybody floated up and down the halls,
wearing their boyfriends.
    At football games you had to have one to get in,
    and also they were required at drive-ins.

The second one was a charm against the common family
evils, and homelessness,
the sin of geography.
I conjured up shelter and years of it
at night in Kansas City or in Canada.
I said to him over and over
that he made me invisible; when they started
for me, I said his name.
I said his name once too often.
These charms get worn like tires.

Sitting one evening in my Witchmobile,
which was an abandoned pickup wrecked
beside the Little Slocan, I lit a
cigarette, and the matchlight shone
on all the rusty dials;
    and the gas said empty,
    and the speed said zero,
    and the engine had no temperature at all,
while at the same time the river drove southward
and it was full and speedy and cold,
and so I said to hell with these dangerous charms,
they backfire, why do I do these things to myself?
I can buy my own clothes and rent my own house,
and you (or somebody looking exactly like you)
came walking out of the river trail, saying *Paulette?*

These are the wings of the airplane.
They have leading edges and cut the air
like a pie-knife through a fine meringue.

These are the struts. They hold the wings to the fuselage;
they correspond to the arms of angels
that you see in ancient paintings,
held out in surprise or warning
against wings with feathers
and no leading edges.

These are the cowlings that cover the engines
and then the propellers,
sun-dogs, solar discs which will drag behind them
the boxy fuselage
full of passengers, babies, canned vegetables
the nurse says we must eat,
sheets of plexiglass, sleeping bags,
a roll of plastic pipe and the rest of us.

These are the skis on which we take off,
smashing across the raftered ice,
their shock absorbers fed up with all this,
both propellers tuned coarse and driving
at the clear air like diamond drills
reaching for altitude, for distance
and a tailwind out of the north.

Kiss off, kiss off, O earth,
O village of earth-folk down below,
waving your puffy-mitt goodbyes,
we are the people of the air.
Here the milk of winter clouds
is churned into our special butter.

Some day when the roads come in
and cars like armadillos
lurch up their frozen byways,

remember we once flew like legends in these frail kites.
Remember us, a boreal airborne royalty.
Remember some of us died.

And these are the dials of the flight deck.
This is the vertical speed indicator,
this is the radar, at night hissing in green sweeps,
the oil pressure and the bank-and-turn.
This is the altimeter which tells us of the earth,
now drawing up in a snowy flow,

where we owe a life, despite the aviation of souls.
We return in our damp fur and parkas
toward an artificial horizon,
to everything that is unjust, unpaid-for and unwarranted,
claimed by our bodies like baggage,
we, the earth-people,
descend again.

My father was an alcoholic when
all he said he wanted to be was
a member of the Elks Club;
but being an alcoholic was more
exciting and more dreadful.

He was never bored. Drunk, yes, but
not bored.

His heart was an XKE, driven at
top speed; life was
the Grand Prix.

The children inherited busted tires
and speeding tickets.
Some of us had to be sold for parts and

put back together in another chassis.

I am repeatedly shot and killed
while looking for the misplaced thoughts
I dropped here yesterday, while hoping to be transported
up to the white heights of the glacier
where it counts. A hippie woman with big bare feet
and toes that all point ahead fists up her bread
in the plastic shack on the shore.
I have missed out on a lot of things,
except these javelins of light thrown one after the other
out of the hard blue mind of the mountains.
The dough folds like brains,
electrified by bready thoughts.
I shoot myself again and again, I am blown away,
rob my own banks, I ambush myself
from behind the driftwood thrown up
here like breast-works; I turn and am suddenly
faced by both barrels, throw up my hands
in complete surrender.
This is the gun story.
Tomorrow it will be knives.
Evening stroll; Kootenay Lake.
The mind springs
out of the traps of caterpillars,
fully armed,
with wings like spinnakers.

Nothing can jar me from this attentive position,
this pen hesitating over the paper
is a cardiogram needle,
the page will be full of spikes
and indications.

You have been held hostage, have you?
Men with knives,
this came after the bullet
through the window and everyone
tried to get in the bathtub.
    Don't worry, my dear, it is their hormones,
they will be taken to jail
and in there
they will have to hold other men hostage
instead of nurses
and the consequences will be worse.
You say you are leaving this goddamned north,
this Frontier City?
Good, I will write that down.
I have no arguments,
only quotes.

Elder Wapiquae will tell me about stars,
this is for the young people
who are forgetting the traditions of their ancestors,
she says they run around and drink
and throw knives at each other.

"Write down what I say: there are three stars together at breakup
time in the spring, they are three people in a canoe. One is a sun,
the other a moon, male and female in perfect balance. The one in the
middle, I forget who it is. God, maybe. It could be the Loon."

I will make sure you appear just as you are
in our pages, no distortion, the hostages, the elder,
those at the wild rice camps and loons and stars.
And all this time (I am sitting here)
my heart is talking to itself,
all its valves and dull arterial thuds,
it is a high-ranking defector,
    under all this nodding and quotes it says,
Listen to me, only to me. Listen.

I imagine a village;
a woman comes out into the dark with a tin lantern
pierced in Moorish designs,
carrying a basin. Out in the dark
are mountains and hashish,
big things with fur.
Her road has been dynamited many times,
these are inaccessible mountains.
This is a fortified village.
Only you who know Morocco in all her smoke and horses
remember this scene, wet, the inn full of men
like small traders wrapped in butcher paper.
Their robes are the wind's tent.
The flame is small and coddled,
precious as a saint's image. What gives this countryside
its peculiarity is that there are no pictures
anywhere, except for the king's. He reigns over
a tortuous kingdom of blood and sand,
far to the south.
Here, in the sweet, cold
mountain night a woman throws out her dishwater
and there on the wind's edge I am blown,
knocking at many doors, not knowing what
it is I want, except in.

This is the soap of the wife.
How serious is her life.
The babies are soapy and earnest,
the husband has been reamed out and cleaned;
his hands rest on the blue-
willow plate, cautious and eager.
His name is Matia and he
has been squeezing the life
out of little fish all day,
dead-tired.
That was the smoke of the husband.
There are two babies and each one
has an eye for lizards.
They have been catching baby-lizards
all day in the dirt.
Chana washes up, she washes
everything,
her yellow dress the color of a bedspread,
the despondent fish,
the coal-oil lamps with their flames
like wet red banners.
Everything is wet, wet,
full of suds!
The housewife claps her
ragged hands.
It's all over.
Everything is pure and sleepy,
the family slides out of sight.

We almost get used to this moving around, the migratory life; cats and dogs cower in the backs of trucks or vans, there are always the last few articles that drive everyone insane, but can't be thrown away; a Mexican poncho which was a gift from a cousin who bought it in the San Diego Navy, a stuffed elephant spilling packing and devoid of plush, the massive maroon of *The World Book*. A new school looms in the south, big as a county jail. I wonder what kind of clothes they're going to want me to wear? It's always like this; secret crushes on boys who wear undershirts and are named Joe Bob in the place behind, and new, terrible half-men in football sweaters named Lonnie in the place coming up. We are like Aztecs. It's because nothing works. We try again. Maybe it will work next time. We are working on a logic of tangible qualities rather than one of propositions, but neither helps when I find myself moving down onto some perfectly innocent small town in Missouri in an avalanche of odds and ends.

We drive through Lake Ozark and Osage Beach, through all those places which smell like good hamburgers and catfish. We are in a Ranch Wago because the N fell off, who knows when. It is laying on the highway somewhere stuttering its one letter over and over as we bear on. The dog pukes in the back. The cat swarms over my shoulder to get at him while he's preoccupied with throwing up. Everyone laughs. This is astoundingly funny. Gypsy and Stonewall fling themselves at each other among jars of pinto beans and *The World Book* and Mexicali ponchos.

I am not really in my right mind here between one town and another, it is that no-time space which terrifies all nomads. We pass Kiddie Jungle Petting Zoos and roadside emporiums, floating dance halls on converted barges. With a sort of teenage sneer I mention that we are also a Kiddie Jungle Petting Zoo but Poppa Daddy stops for coffee and doesn't want to hear another word out of me.

How about if I write you a note, I think to myself, but me and my sister begin to fight, a real death-struggle, mortal combat, over who gets how many soda pops.

I see the dining emporiums, they are like visions. I wish I was in there with a big straw picture hat and a dress with white shoulder straps, among people I do not know personally and will never know personally. Therefore I will appear among them mysteriously. Their names will be Lonnie and Duane and Joe Bob. They will not know I lurch around Missouri in dented Ranch Wagos full of household pets and tennis shoes and cooking utensils. I am thirteen or fourteen now, sometimes twelve, but like the family abode I shift here and there with amazing rapidity.

I am emerging from this move, the beans-and-poncho move, with a deep regard for this Ozark stopping place where we have halted, suddenly seized with a keen desire for a life of degeneracy among the floating dance halls. There are two of me, and one of them says *keep them happy* and the other says *jump from the car now, emerge as only you can by falling from a speeding object, quick, before we gain too much momentum.*

Ah, but here comes Poppa Daddy back with the coffee and Nehis and all the gates shut up on the lidless world. There will be no jumping from doors or hats or catfish. There is a town a hundred miles from here where we will arrive and unload beans and everything.

On the other hand, my sister and I have already heard the music. It is our music, they were playing our song in there. It is as if in some other time-warp there is a roadside emporium for each one of us, whose music is always playing at the back of our minds, a sort of celestial roadhouse, a cosmic bar and grille with Bar-B-Q and windows that look out on a river, and the waitress knows your name. In the confines of the worried mind you can go there and order whatever your heart desires; if you are on speaking terms with your heart, if you know the names of your desires. Maybe they will be printed on the menu.

And, as in dreams when we recognize perfect strangers, we will know everybody there. They will say, where have you been so long? And you think up some excuse: I was lost in the upper reaches of the Orinoco, maybe, or I had a hot date in Hong Kong. Inside each one of us it's always Amateur Night at the Dixie Bar and Grille.

We drive away from the Jim'N'Judy Starlight Cafe and Dancing Sat. Nites, my sister and I stare at each other, we are not smiling but.

The beauty of landscapes is a great stimulus.
Even the real-estate sign across the street
lighting up the front room like persistent heat-lightning.

And the streetcars creep by catlike on unbending rails
cracking electrical walnuts, blue-white and dangerous.

A headful of voltage,
a long trip to the end of town.

I

We are coming up the highway at top speed,
we have a message to deliver;
the message is this:

Everything is out of control.
Cars tear past
    my mare has gone through the bit and
can't be stopped or turned
    at the top of this hill,
we will meet a logging truck.
It will be a surprise,
the driver
    will say O
        no,
so will I. The horse says nothing;
they never do.
    I remember now,
it was to be memorized
    and not written down
in case the enemy.
You can let go now.

2

Later I can lay on a hospital bed
    and think about things.
I have a stunning concussion.
We are small, small I tell you,
    among all these animals.
We can be thrown great distances,
we bounce when we hit.
    You stand several miles away

at the bedside
and grip my hand.

We will come to this final parting too,
    it will be similar,
the same charge and wind
and fear of dying, a separation,
    the slow wheel in mid-air, maybe
we can fly after all,
    the same (O

no) impact and pain arriving
like sirens.
Afterward we lay like a thrown rag.
I almost feel happy.
You can let go now.

This is a song for people who lie
at the bottom of the deep ocean of their minds and can't
sing. Overhead the thoughts plow like tankers, hard
and determined, on their way to a port where they
will be unloaded and then turn to sea again; it is
endless. The crew has not had liberty in years. Down
in the deep Atlantic caverns are other ships, in worse
condition.

The mind is dense as water and can't be compressed.
For the big thoughts that plunge on like cargo ships,
the mind is only an impediment; it's something in the way
between one secure shore and another, they want
to get through it and as fast as possible. These
are songs for people who would rather think like
yachts, for people who are in love with the sky.
Like sailors they look at the sky first thing in
the morning and they do their singing for
themselves. Sky, give me good wind and some fair weather.
They believe naturally in big things.

This is a song for people who have come from a long
way off, through equinoctial storms, and are drenched
even under the foul-weather gear, who have jury-
rigged everything, whose lockers have flown open
under the crash of the washerwoman wind, black as
a hammer with rain; and the mustard and the soup and
dehydrated onions are all over the bunks, and the
cabin sole is a foot under water; people who slide
in under a descending sky and you see them coming
into harbor; somebody is standing out on the forepeak
with a line to throw to you, there on the dock. They
look blank. They have said all the prayers they know

and have begun to repeat themselves. Maybe they have
a story to tell. Maybe they can't even speak.

This is a song about people who think like squids
or jellyfish, a demand inhabits them the way
a hermit crab inhabits a shell, and with their great
red claws they slowly take something apart. When
their thoughts touch you, you try to get out of
the way. Sing from a distance. Think of having
something like this for a parent. This is also a
song for the children, who are often eaten or
stung, who float in the waves like mermaids,
calling for help, dangerous and irresistible.

My brain, this tramp steamer, grinds on, loaded
with facts. I would like to find the port where
I am to dump everything and unload, all the ore pellets
roaring down the chutes, or the freon cold of
liquefied natural gas being piped off into shore
facilities. Then I would hijack my ship and
turn to sea again, to Greenland or the Windward
Islands, I would give the crew all their hard-
earned liberty, we would sail under our own
flag, we would survive everything, rolling with the
tides of the mind and all its punches, the
risky ventures. Blue hurricanes.
O the bounty of the mutiny.

This is a song for privateers.

The earth folds up her grasses.
Starshine strikes like the appearance of aliens.
The aurora is a piano, playing blues
in green neon. The junked taxi sinks
into the asters.

In the center of all this noisy brilliance
is a cabin; silence and absence.

Sometimes you spoon-feed the soul,
silence in small sips,
a sort of dole, you
put it on relief.

Foxtail grass turns gravely on its spears.
Shut up, wait for the angel or the airplane
disguised as an angel to descend
with silent twin propellers out of the
madonna-blue evening, wait for
your cue, your
moment to appear in the
zodiacal footlights of
this special and dreadful
one-man show.

Married men,
their rings, their wives,
their other lives.

She's asleep in a barrel
at home,
polishing the Mouchas
and the Wittgensteins.

The hours and minutes are frozen in trays.
No change in the weather for days and days.
She runs after him with a tube.
He beats her off with a rake.

From these deaths of fog and machinery
    we hope to excuse ourselves.
Your news arrives on the wings of voices.
    We are awakened from our daily bath.

In the metal confetti
which was the airplane,
    the village people walk around confused,
their lives in their hands.
    Pieces of instruments lay hopeless in the snow.
In this there is neither
    philosophy nor solutions,
only loss; four children, two adults.
Something arrived in the air

like a revelation,
and then disintegrated.
It happens too fast to understand what was said
or meant
and it is not in our language.

It is not in any language.
For years they will piece together small events,
looking for clues,
the conclusions will be bound and distributed.
They think they know already; so do we,

but no one will second-guess
what might be found
in these hard-bound volumes of snow and gasoline
and fire.
O pilot error, the last judgment.

Without clothes, we burn like candles, our veins close
to the surface, and weeks later we begin to shine.
*"It's not myself, but something in the universe
I have been left with."*

I

This is a cedar swamp. He is in here somewhere,
on aluminum snowshoes, a fresh trail and clouds
of nicotine streaming behind like smoke flares;
in search.

Lost children (some ran away), drunks falling
into ravines, midnight farmers out loose
in the sleet-slick fields in search of suicide,
a man with a shotgun
and eyes full of firepower.
These are his clues.

He moves on the edges like a roll of dimes
or something hungry. There are false starts,
midnight alarms.

He lives for the moment;
he talks the knife away
from the suicide man,
a flash of checkered shirt
at the bottom of a ravine,
the second when the child in the clearing
turns and cries out,
still alive.

The drunk and the suicide
and the Roadhouse Mystery Killer
are erratic and snaky,
they are the gothics,
hates and divorces, moon revenges.
They are petrified of the dog.

They could be anywhere,
but he always

finds the child exactly in the center of the world.

2

What if you were lost in this cedar swamp—
you would shout and then scream, after a while
you would become childlike, you would forget
all the numbers

that have been assigned to you,
your telephone number,
social security, driver's license,
the arguments with your loved one
would evaporate,
you would forget
your first name
and then your last name,

and every direction would be the wrong one
so directions would cease.
You would be at the hub of the universe
and around you, in every direction,
the world. As you finally give up hope,
you become the eye
of creation.

Then he would arrive, crashing
through the rigid, thorned sticks,

bringing with him all the numbers,
the arguments, the first and last names,
your identity
whether you want it or not.

Maybe you don't want it anymore.
He knows this.
He has found lots of children.
When the sergeant goes home at dawn
he looks like he has just come back
from the center of the earth,

the hard way,
by way of a town called Argus
in Egremont Township,
where all the murderers live.

Hunger can destroy anything,
takes pity on nothing.

I have dreams of India when
the wild men emerge like sticks
and their shoulders are nothing
and their eyes are a maw
their bodies a stitch between two vacuums.

On my empty bottle sits
a wild globe of fire; like the sea
I am vacant.

That life might nourish me with this starvation;
that after the empty heart
would come understanding.

My aunts washed dishes while the uncles
squirted each other on the lawn with
    garden hoses. Why are we in here,
I said, and they are out there?
    That's the way it is,
    said Aunt Hetty, the shriveled-up one.

I have the rages that small animals have,
being small, being animal.
    Written on me was a message,
"At Your Service,"
like a book of paper matches.
One by one we were taken out
and struck.
    We come bearing supper,
our heads on fire.

White as cave fish my blind legs
creep out of their jeans; snow white and
there are seven dwarves who live in my
dresser sorting clothes,
losing things.
    They are my tiny mythologies
and what they know they never tell.

It takes days to get people out of my head
—the huntsman, the woman with the mirror—
dwarves like days of the week take on
names and disappear.

Someday the prince will come
splashing across Crawford Creek carrying
the mail; he will walk up the
sand bank past the disintegrating
chickenhouse and the pile of discarded lumber.
He will be carrying junk mail from all
the alternative universes, an invitation to
a ball in Babylon IV.
I will be sitting outside peeling poisonous apples
    arguing in my head with the
mad huntsman, the woman with the sinister mirror.
    I don't know if I will see him
or not, but
    I think so.

The dwarves will see him.
The dwarves see everything.

We are flying directly into darkness, the
dim polestar rides on the starboard wing,
Orion and his blue gems freeze in the southwest.

Our rare and singular lives are in the hands of the pilot;
after him the radar and one engine.
There were two engines when we started out
but the other one died.

We watch the starboard propeller feather
in slow, coarse revolutions.
The pilot says we will make Attiwapiskat or some place.
          Icarus, our pilot and our downfall.

Two thousand feet below, dim lakes pour past
as if on their way to a Laundromat.
How could we have sunk so low?
At times like this I consider life after death
as if it were a binary system;
there are no half-lives.
We track cautiously down the Milky Way,
home of nebulae and Cygnus.

We are footloose in the corridors of the aurora.

The long stream of my life is flying out
behind this airplane like skywriting
on the subarctic night, fluttering,
whipped with urgency.
Each episode was always cut off from the last,
I used to find myself a series of hostile strangers,
startled in doorways.

Now they gather themselves up,

the wives, daughters, friends, victims, perpetrators,
the one with the pen and the other carrying a blank mask,
another at present at the cleaners.

They catch up and slam together like
a deck of cards, packed into the present
moment.
I draw one out; it's the ace of airplanes.
The radar repeats a fixed,

green idea. The pilot feels for the radio touch
of Thunder Bay.

At a thousand feet we make quick decisions
about our loyalties, the other engine might fail,
the suitcases of our hearts might be opened
with all that contraband,
the jewels and screams,
we might have things to declare;
         the universe is my native country
         poetry is my mother tongue
         the ideas I have purchased on this side
of the border don't amount to
more than a hundred dollars.
What comes after this?

What do you mean, what comes after this?
This is it.
Attiwapiskat approaches, a Cree village
on a cold salt coast, flying patchwork quilts
in several more colors than are found in nature,
shining with blue-white runway lights.

We will sleep in the guesthouse tonight,

that refuge of displaced persons.
The pilot will go down and repair the valve
and say nothing happened.
(We flew into darkness at the rim of the world,
where distant lights broke through
and something failed us.
Then at the edge when we were stamped
and ready to go through we were turned back.)
We can unload and forget it.
But I will remember
and then go back and forget again.
This is Attiwapiskat, everything is as it should be.
We slide down to the airstrip through salt fogs
from Hudson Bay that slip through the night
like airborne bedsheets.
We get off, still life with sleeping bags.
Approaching us is an earthman,
speaking Cree.

I wrote you last night and the night before.
You know your attention
turns me navy-blue. I am a horse once in a while
and run like thundering barrels for whatever horizon
offers itself. These poems pile up.
A catbird sings in her green tree,
the sun filters down to a chemical green.
A wire in the shape of a permanent wave is
being installed between here and the next town.

Over this wire I can talk to the image of
a Spanish marine, holding his fine white hat,
at any moment of the day or night.
I didn't want these images,
I didn't want them like that.
If only a companion would pour himself
into my glittering glass
and the roads return my lost change.

There go the bells again. They are striking Angelus in
the middle
of the night.
My three silver rings perch
on my fingers and shine like gin.
They ride in
at the end of this line,
stabled and fine, my white horses.

The cabin is dipped in darkness, tie-dyed.
Only the red from the woodstove grate and reflections

on tin plates escape. Sirius picks at the window. Diapers wave
at half-mast, desperately clean. The children watch

the insides of their eyes. Things will be revealed in dreams
to them, economy-sized revelations, tiny ideas.

The body shuts down. Hot pine ticks in the stove.
We sleep because we have to dream, as when

we are awake we must speak. Speech and dreams;
behind the banner of these old imperatives we

have marched for two million years, to what
(unspeakable) end? On the banks of the Severn

River and the subarctic night; and now one of the
children calls out sharply, ambushed by dreams.

This is Sunday morning, July 16, 1958, Cole Camp, Butler County, Missouri, population 100 and just look at all these people getting ready for church. We are only 150 miles from the Arkansas border down here, which seems to loom dangerously close. Whatever bad happens, happens to the south of us. There are too many layers of dresses but it seems I and every other teenage girl down here have been hired to play extras in *Gone With the Wind*. There are hot irons and potentially torn nylons. The tar on county road double E helplessly melts in the furnace of July, decorated with squashed, imbedded salt-and-pepper king snakes.

In the hot, expanding morning I rise up over the necks of dresses like yeast dough, and precisely the same color. Hooks and eyes and zippers, the garter belts and elastic waists of petticoats, everything needs repairing and stitching and hooking up.

The men dress in simple, decent clothes, my brother Elroy is absorbed in the mysteries of the Windsor knot. Their pants are held up by brown and honest belts which require no more than the brains of a two-year-old to fasten.

But I am educated, I have spent hours in the encyclopedia, I know that South American Indian men in *The World Book* are the ones who decorate themselves; they spend hours painting their faces and stick bird of paradise feathers through their noses. Did you hear that? Is she talking? Never mind, Poppa Daddy, she just said something about somebody having a bird of paradise feather up their nose.

I look at my ironed and lacy dress laid out on the bed and I really want to be neolithic and hulk around the village in primitive weaves with beads made out of rocks and zircons. No dice, not in this town. The high heels now after six months' wear have scraped off their heel caps, the forefoot bulges out, full of big and little toes, the points bend up like coffeepot spouts. Does God really want us to wear this crap? In the blue-hot morning the bells ring and ring.

Down the road the Pentecostals weep and howl and walk into walls, but only on special occasions. In our Baptist church, which is the established one of the region, there will be only moderate demands at the end of the sermon for sinners to come up and repent with everybody looking at you and thinking about your clothes and what you have done in them. Thoughts like lint in the pockets and linings.

Meanwhile we sweat and fan ourselves with Jesus fans, sing, twist around on the pews. The starched laces cut into my thighs until they look like basketweave and I hope nothing gives way. There is so much that *can* give way, therefore it will; the zipper of this too-tight bodice, the treacherous garter belt, the perilous elastics of petticoats. Only the big, serious girdle with its rubberized tube will hold out, despite everything, to the very end. They will bury me in the god-damned thing.

(Out of this green and steaming town I suspect there are other modes of existence. A Cherokee woman appears out of history, displaced and immediate, walking through New Echota in the early morning. She is surrounded by several vital colors and the air is red with morning. In her basket are blue things, spirits, green corn, a white luna moth, animal pelts. But history shuts her down; they are moving up even now, animal crackers from Georgia in stolen uniforms.)

We walk to church. I am in the center of innumerable systems, a complex machine. All around me women are trying to elevate like floating ice creams despite the heat, and the iron lace, and the hooks. They are possessed with themselves and well they ought to be, the center of complex and disintegrating systems constantly in repair. (Can man be saved? the preacher asks, which means I have to think this out by myself, single-handed.) (No.) Explore nothing. Develop a pleasing manner. Contemplate your tubes.

In the Sunday-school class for young adults we play riddle games. What is a woman's crowning glory, asks the teacher, who is the lady that operates the town switchboard. I think desperately of crown and head and then I say hair. No, ha ha, it is her son! Son-sun, get it? Elroy smirks from behind his Windsor knot. Somehow I know this doesn't work out. Is something wrong with my hair? Why do I take this so seriously? All this hot Sunday I take seriously the dreadful, precarious system of female clothes and shoes, the green, sizzling Ozarks, the white frame church and its eloquent bells, the Jesus fans and the overhead fans. Thut, thut, thut, they have one word, maybe it is the word of surrender or praise, perhaps it is the slow chorus of a world of eternal Sunday; the madhouse.

Outside a line of hills runs by, throwing treats and leaves. Turn-back Creek boils with springwater, the crawdads celebrate Sunday and escape several raccoons. A cave opens its mysterious interior for visitors. Corn patches reflect a team of suns and the cobs fuse. There is some maroon music being played, elegantly, with hautboys and a viola da gamba in the shade of the chinquapin trees.

Sometimes we carry our souls in our fists, tightly, against those who would extract them from us, like a storekeeper gently extracting pennies from the fists of children at Loller's station where we used to stop on the way to church, to buy candy with our plate money; and we wanted the candy but we would not give up the pennies either; and what you have to do is open your fist, and it will suddenly spring up like a luna moth; and then you are on the road to New Echota, which leads through mountain valleys, at the thirty-sixth parallel, and you will be transfixed by a fox looking at you out of the jewelweed, who has just darted out of your heart and into the world. It is no smaller nor any happier than any other fox, or any other heart-bearing ore, red as Iron Mountain, and he or she will disappear like an idea into the world of legends; the thick shushing of fans reminds us we are in church, worshipful. What will it avail a woman if she gain her own mind but lose her soul? All right, I will lose my soul. Not once but a hundred times. As many times as it takes. Turn now to page 145 and sing are you washed in the blood. No.

I used to be paranoid,
thinking someone was after me,
but it was you all along.

This is a dead end street.
Smooth buildings loom
and look the other way.
I will spike you with my needle heels,
I will call the morality police,
the troops, the army,
the guerrillas, whoever it is
that sees to these things.

It's hopeless.
Police don't come to domestic quarrels anymore,
they are always getting shot.
People who love each other
are dangerous;
the only thing between them
is a field of fire.
And I forgot,
you are the police.

First they want you to come in
    for observation, they want to know
if you are crazy or depressed.
If they think you are crazy
then you have to wear pajamas all day
and make things out of clay
and take drugs.
    These drugs make each day hotter
than the day before
and then
    they turn up the thermostat.
    If you are crazy
you have to go in your bathrobe
and talk to men who are in suits and ties.
They want to know if you are hearing things
    besides them.

If they consider you are crazy
you will be given more drugs
and asked to play netball.
    If you are only depressed
then you may have
both drugs and clothes;
they don't really want you.
Depressed people are predictable,
it's always money or love,
likely both.
    People have always been terrible
to depressives; the truly mad
take it all on themselves—
    the drugs, the bathrobes,
    the clay pots, the netball.
They believe everything, like puppies.

They are the true soldiers of this white, hot
    barracks.
The rest of us are draft-dodgers,
conscientious objectors.
We watch like people at an accident,
    their long dismantling.

A LETTER TO MY GRANDAD ON THE OCCASION OF A LETTER FROM COUSIN WANDA LEE SAYING GRANDAD IS TOO INFIRM TO FEED THE COWS AND IS NOT LONG FOR THIS WORLD

Wanda Lee says you follow her around like an old pup
when she comes to visit.
You were the one who blinded a mule with a bramble
stick in 1911, pulled three children from a
burning tent in 1937, knocked Wanda Lee's boyfriend
down for saying shit in 1946 and now she says
you've had it.
She expects to remember all the proper things and cry,
spontaneously, at your waxed and flowered figurine
and the dirt they throw you in.
She primes herself, imitating your geriatric bent,
swelling with emotions like a revivalist's tent.
You liked the gentler music, with Dobro and
mouth harp, especially "Traveler's Lament."
I won't visit your already-divided homestead,
or help you feed the cows,
or stir your muddy ears with shouts.
I won't be coming to your funeral, so
so long for now.
You knock me out.
Remember our secret,
remember our secret.

In the legends, it's always like this:
still water, one person alone on a beach,
    oppositions silently sliding
on each other like the two arguments
of an earthquake,
its inevitable faults.
The mountains move in and out of clouds
like secret doctrines.
Red willows line up on the sand,
not speaking to one another,
and like this they have spent the night,
and the morning,
and their entire lives.

After long silences, speech appears
like a voice from a red willow bush, burning:
I love you, or
The bread pans are on that shelf,
or I am afraid of dying.

At one in the morning,
poetry fastens with clean, desperate hands
on my nightgown, saying
Say this, say this, this is
the perfect thing to say.
And then whole lines arrive,
whispering modestly
Say me.

The Waterloo Express is big and important with its
glass eye, the eye of a fanatic. Sometimes they are

so important they pass you by, headed for a great
destination and bending the rails into a pure musical phrase.

Snatched loose from my baggage and address, goodbyes falling
away in flakes of dead skin, you'd say I was a high

pariah, sleepless and nowhere to go. Who do you think
I am? I bet you think I'm running away from home or

a man who never done me wrong. I bet you think
I'm twenty, with the fragile soul of a wild fawn.

Well, I used to think so too, but the job didn't pay much
and anyhow I never liked the taste of wages.

I like it here in the middle element where this
express is ripping up the dawn like an old ticket

whose engine is blowing the towns away
and even I am barely holding on.

There they go—a toe, a finger, my coat—honey,
you'd hardly recognize me, pared down to one white eye.

It has the cynical glint of a dynamite salesman.

Everybody has parents, even parents.
There is the Family Novel
in which they are all children,
only some are more powerful than others.
Getting money out of parents
has become harder lately;
they claim they have spent their allowances
and won't share their Sweet Maries.
On deserted streets,
kicking piles of chestnut leaves,
your mother comes home from school
late and reluctantly.

Honey, you know when you talk like that
you're the only man I'll ever love.
Just keep talking.
That's what you're good for.
Over your voice my mind
snaps taut as a sheet in a high wind.
Here you have my history
written in the text of my left hand.

I am on my feet for another year
and the next one after that.
Just keep talking.
That's what you're good for.
I am quiet, quiet,
listening for a step at the door,
the approach of morning.

This is where the English came and fortified
themselves against Lake Michigan, Chippewas, wolves,
the French, rebellions. The walls are white as
the Caribbean, the water is the same blue
but more glacial. Young men walk around in
pipe-clayed britches and fire off muzzle-loaders.
People scream. Everything is like it was.

In the bay below the walls, our boat nods
like a gull in the middle of expensive
racers, ocean-goers, hundred-footers.
We stopped talking somewhere
around Sault Ste. Marie.

On the docks men are using wagons and
big Belgian horses to off-load ice cream
and asphalt. No cars are allowed on this
island. You're waiting for me to ask what's
the matter. I played that game already. So
has everybody. No surrender.

I'm glad we sailed here; there are all kinds
of lessons about people who
guard themselves behind walls and are
defeated by treachery, they get you
when your guard is down, the night watch
hopes his cigarette will burn his lips if
he falls asleep, the innocent enemy playing lacrosse
in front of the gates, then the bloodshed
and men hiding in pork barrels.

If only we could arrange to leave each
other simultaneously, without the war, with
a small, sharp noise like a halyard parting in

mid-wind, if only we knew how to make love,
piece by piece, out of common household materials.

If we knew how the pieces fit, how
it worked. War is easier. One or the
other will win, leave first, sign things,
move out.

You build the walls first. After the
fortifications are ready, then you get
your French, your wolves, your
Chippewas and rebellions. No chance to
get the message through, the runners wash
up on the shore months later.

We sail past the ferryboat, the only
sound is the wind's slow whistle,
the boom of the evening cannon, and
a crowd of people presenting arms.

My sister Sunny,
   youngest of all the family daughters,
walking in the St. Louis heat,
the scattered, late magnolia.
   White petals fly past us,
a diplomat is shredding his codes,
his unlucky history.

   She is thin and precarious in bright cotton,
pneumonia lives next door,
   they exchange coughs. We have no family policies,
we are caught between trying to repair
   everything and throwing it away.
Don't die yet, we just started.

   My mother walks with her,
an heirloom of the wars,
both of them are minor heatwaves.
They have a splendid flash.

   At the door to the great river
we watch our lives rush downstream
   in the April floods, chicken coops,
old arguments, accusations, outhouses,
the gates of vanished fences.
   So this is life, we say,
this is not bad,
give us more of this thunder,
   the floods, the buoyant paddlewheelers.
Give us not only this day
   but the next.

In this dream we have the mysteries
of the moon's confusions.
People pass by on the snowy road
followed by the luminous morse of lightning bugs.
Several feet behind them
    drift their voices.
    Maybe they will sue somebody,
maybe not.
    "We never knew it was dependency," they say.
"We thought it was love."
    Who would have told us otherwise?
They pass by, unidentifiable, familiar,
carrying torches of regret.
We all thought it was love,
    everything was love
except love,
and that
    was only passion.

Spring spikes all this aloneness with surprise flowers.
I am attacked by birds, sharp grass.
Psychiatrists talk to us for nothing
on days like this.

    Nature is another dimension
and it is like talking to Martians,
    walking by the dry roadside I am passed
by a lot of cars, all of them dusty,
filled with farm implements,
parts to make the world go,
    to make everything operate all right,
open and bloom and take root.
    It's a dry spring this year.
Water haunts the ditches like anti-matter.

    You up there,
face in the clouds,
you seem tired,
like a first wife.
They didn't talk to you either,
it got wordless like this,
didn't it?

The bells of Mass state their names and conditions.
They have been hung alive
by their voices in the belfry.
There is so much grief in what they say.
The church is an Arabian structure
domed and palmy against the cliffs.
Its pure white is a work of love.
They are first of a stairwell, these domes,
mounting perfectly in their address to heaven.

I am memorizing my sins,
most of all my memories of him,
of his suffering magnitude
like a crowd of Lutherans in church.
How I used to love it!
I fell in love with the reports, the promises,
assumptions on my part
on my part
on my own most grievous part.

The Mass is a woman.
She is wild with blemishes.
Is she too big?
Can she get her arms around God?
She offers a false body
to fend off hope;
and this is how we eat it,
sick with what we have swallowed.

In the kitchen everything happens; at least twice. I sit at the table (it is dinnertime) and read about cave-people and how they started making copper things. Dinner is partially large pieces of Velveeta cheese and I say "copper" to myself because it sounds weird with cheese in my mouth. Forever after I associate copper and cheese.

And there is noise and people as there always is (I have escaped you ha! even though I sit here). Cute Mom says do you have to read *all* the time? Big cave-men in fur diapers and Naugahyde jumpsuits beat out orangey lumps of what looks like stale Velveeta cheese. I gaze at them from afar through the windows of this book and its amateur illustrations. Even I know the anatomy is wrong. For once I see myself in repose. Around me people are yelling in defensive and accusative tones; in declarative sentences, imperatives, shrieks. Poppa Daddy threatens to hit everyone and probably will (it will, after all, restore order) and tells Cute Mom to get him something. A glass of water. An electric fan. A spoon. Deep in the book more cave-men advance with copper tools, they evidently hammered them out in the space of two pages. I think about being a cave-person as a career but there are no girls in all these cold-forged tools and women appear only in the background with baskets, which are evanescent in the course of history and rot quickly. I imagine myself making whatever living I can in solitude with nothing but baskets, it won't be easy, I have begun to realize the world goes better with people who bash things than with people who carry things in baskets. I see double or on several planes at once; cheese, copper, potato soup, Big Jim and Sparky who are pure sound out of the radio, hairy women lurking in shadow, electric fans, Cute Mom talking in an undertone to the cat.

Bert the female parakeet storms across the table, dragging her tail through the fried eggs. Poppa Daddy begins to tell Cute Mom about someone he welded the frame on a truck for down in Butler County and she should get him a clean shirt. Dong the cave-adolescent stumbles into volcanic fire and decides this is the Fire-God. Good thinking, Dong. My brother rushes outside, away from the mad kitchen and its random occurrences. He pumps up his BB gun and shoots the neighbor kid in the leg.

Dong has now discovered metallurgy and cries aiee! as he drops molten copper on his foot. The police arrive. Did your son shoot somebody in the leg? You bet. The police!! Everybody hides. The authorities! Dong has, then, discovered both metallurgy and cheese-product. Lightning strikes the tribal camp and blows the fur diapers all to flinders and thus they discover fused things. They all cry "Lightning-God!" What with this and the Volcano-God they have discovered religion, too, but it appears to me they will all go to hell anyway as they are not Baptists. Too bad for you, Dong.

The mind can do several things at once, but none of them very well. It can, if pressed, operate on three or four levels and not one of these levels is the real level, the real head, the genuine and certifiable self. Dong, too, stumbles on burnt-sienna spearheads through the land of glaciers, gathering his responses for the next chapter, cold as Zen. Poppa Daddy and Elroy are out on the porch and Poppa Daddy shouts, forcing Elroy to bash his BB gun to bits on the porch rail. This will teach him to shoot thick, pale neighbor kids in their thick, pale legs. The police have retired from the scene. They got embarrassed. As who wouldn't? Elroy is wretched, he believes it all; he thinks this is him, smashing his beloved weapon to death on the porch rail. I will have more potato soup and cheese; we are too little to go to prison at any rate.

We have many names for ourselves but none of them is the real name. Call us by our real name (beloved) and we will fire up like forges, among books or glaciers, in police stations, in the kitchen of the asylum, we will hear it as if someone (beloved) had left a mist on the glass panes of our souls with a secret breath. The name which will pull us out of every context, replacing us with a newer and thinner personage who will be us, after all.

I will finally raise my head from this book to look you in the face in your paleolithic furs and desperate tools and say (beloved) your name as well.

I

In a city like this, the citizens dream of light—
chemical fogs burn with sulphur, bursting the molecules
of water,
and the dry, pearl-colored sheet of cloud
that is always drawn over Toronto in a modest way;
lights of mussel-shell and stained ash, lights
on the edges
of metal cans and the sparkling oil of garbage
soaking the alley soil;
reflections from the metal hooks of a public character
tapping down Adelaide.

In a city like this, the citizens wake up on time
smashing the morning alarm and swallowing
the coffee pot that stains their mirrors with steam.

II

In Ontario they grow truck-farms;
furrows sprout scissors
cigar-tins, saucers of salt
scraps of cigarette packages
canceled stamps, old address-books
pencils with the erasers chewed off.

III

Deeper in the soil grow onion-butts
winding translucent layers of skin around themselves.
A corona of hair-roots composed
of chains of single cells

is spreading to other continents.
Garlic cannot contain itself and its urgent,
    lemonshaped sections.
Carrots refract orange signals into the
    surrounding sediment.
Beneath the soil someday they will uncover
    a crowd
that was digging its way to the Gobi.
They will have become concrete
and dry dirt will fall off them in clods
as they are resurrected,
under a sky whose revolutions
are slow as condensations;
whose horizon gets thumbed open
into white pages.

My sleeping bag used to belong to a pilot who
crashed and died of it.
I didn't know this when I bought it.
It still wants to get up and fly away
seduced by its own goose down
still stained with gas and oil which
airplane wrecks splash out for hundreds of
yards around.
It came to me half-price,
ashamed of its past,
looking for a new owner,
the hieroglyphs of disaster
written on its zipper bag
in engine oil.
Come here and I'll hold you, I said:
we lay wrapped on the cabin floor
all night at bush camp.

The northern lights flared, they made
searchlights throughout Lyra and Scorpio looking
for the plane.
I coughed badly in the early morning like
a faulty engine.
People emerged from my dreaming speaking
perfect Cree
the voices of the living woke me and we landed safely,
alive again.

You have to be careful as a white-gloved evidence man,
picking among strands of carpet, specks of plaster,
the piercing shatters of glass
and particles of heart shattered.

In the litter of real things
there are arcane meanings
in laundry markings,
notepaper pressed with overwriting,
words that were never said out loud
are found in big packages
like marked bills
or gelignite.

This is going to all fit together;
we will get a time and a place,
a description, a face,
we need an argument
overheard by the pizza delivery boy
to establish motive,
we need some blood.

But if I bend to you like a tender commissioner,
if I say, we have the facts already,
we can place you there at the time,
you have the motive,
would you give me
one of those true confessions?
I don't want any more cop novels,
detective mysteries,
I just want it straight
from your hot lips.

Wake up, will you? and get
out of bed.
There are twenty-seven different ways
to kill an outlaw, and I know
every one of them.
There was that sordid hotel in
Frobisher Bay and the singing Greenlanders,
also the twin otter flying low and
heavy over the Hudson Straits; you were
reading a spy novel while I sat in the tail
section and shook, looking down at
the traveling pack ice.

You said you could swim in the Arctic Ocean
and survive and you did. It's all in
knowing how to live you said;

wake up, you have half an hour
before plane time,
before you leave
I want to know your secret.

WHO CAN SAY

Who can say what bitter messages the mail from home will bring?
"We'd better go on," I said, "the end is coming soon in a red
package."
Or like the sentence of a long afternoon which will not end
but, like the sea, stays always at our left hand
traveling south to Perpignan.

A rainstorm flew over, beating its wings and cawing, forced
to earth by a heavy downdraft.
The wind draws itself up to a great height, shot with dust and empty
cigarette packages. It fell on us
as we joined up with a mail train moving south.

IT IS THE SECOND

It is the second of February at 2:35 in the morning as I write this
with a peculiar hand that seems to belong neither to me nor anyone
but whose genuine allegiance is probably to Charlton Heston,
cowering nations under his heel and an untamed woman in his arms.
Outside my windows the cactus of Provence embrace each other
in a spiny, penetrating clasp.
A waiter, newly washed and wrung out, is hanging on the roof to dry,
ready for the morning.
He snaps in the breeze and his opalescent freshness
reminds me of you.
You know I'd just as soon be in Waterloo without a dime
than sitting here breathing this salty air which is filled
like fiberglass
with innumerable slivers and cactus spines.

I WAS DETERMINED

I was determined to report back to you. I am lost on the road.
These silences jam the mind like radar; staccato silence,
the holes between Morse Code . . . containing a message.
    (That was the message.)
The Guardia Civil destroys my careful packing.
I knew them by the eagles on their belts. Their belts creak.
They found out how empty, empty I was and the French said
"If we'd known how empty you were without him
we wouldn't have bothered."
St. Theresa keeps wanting to fight with them and I have a hard time
getting her out of bars.
The land is a carved thing, yellow and still. It has no voice
    and its breath
is an empty wind, the same one that followed us on the mail train,
A Sephardic fairy tale, reminding, reminding.

THE NIGHT MANAGER

The Night Manager has a hard time managing his nights.
My shoes hid under the bed,
tying and untying themselves in a fit of nerves waiting
for me to do something
to heal myself, to put my feet in them
in a gesture of trust and familiarity and move on.

The Night Manager does a poor job with his dreams.
You'll have to line up for tickets and they'll cost you.
You could end up with a nightmare or a fever,
your blankets on the floor and the temperature thirty-five degrees.

I sat in front of the Water Cathedral, the Archangel Gabriel
or one of those flushed, brassy messengers coming and going
    like an advertisement,
hoping I'd remember you. I was striking the hour, my heart gone out
to reminiscence and noonday on my mind
when the Night Manager woke me up and wanted his dream back.
It was midnight.
My brain, St. Theresa later informed me, was at that point
a black tide which broke from my throat
turning night into day
and its depths contained the green, oily slick of phosphorus.

1922, now there was a year.
How did anyone get through it?
It must have crystallized into
a million tiny habits, like nuns.
3:45 p.m. December 18, 1922, or
2:01 a.m. May 3, 1922, and
so on.

How did it get to be 6:42 a.m.
September 10, 1968?
Here I am twenty-five
and I'm tired of it already.

The mind recuperates slowly, it takes a while.
Slowly turning in its nest at night,
it wonders, yes, it wonders,
it has its doubts.

The brain is something else.
In the morning it turns on
like a lightbulb,
the tongue like a chain unleashing it,
prepared for the radio-shack and the powder snow:
turn on the transmitter, broadcast brain-music.

The mind is more admirable and more bruised.
Sometimes it will not appear at all,
sluggish and offended. There is nothing you can
offer it but the situation.
The brain is happy with anything.

As in families or short-run ferries we seem
to move in ever-widening circles.
Maltese mechanics operate the Toronto Island ferries,
running through their hands like docking lines
an intimate knowledge of large
bodies of water.
Ice splinters all over the lake as we argue through
and over the distances between Front Street and America
the sounds pour out like primal causes.

Passengers, tired as old eyes,
lost spectacles on the deck, walking on total recall
dangerous as water,
reflecting on their former lives.
As everything became former
the minute we cast off.
Like coins we lived in the
purse of the city;
searchlights on the water look for
our previous lives;

nighttime travelers on a lake
the color of outer space.

The night wind is big and noisy.
There are no lost souls talking in it, there is nobody,
just the voice of the highway—
the white dotted lines are a snowstorm
that melts in the radiator.
In front of an engine like this anger folds up,
a weak flame, the gas all gone and evaporated.
Is it a tent, instead, the wind?
Not an opening, but an enclosure,
sure and firm.

Its windy folds are innocuous, they will not hurt anyone,
the meteors that streak down are a claw mark
to be closed out or marked shut.
It was the talk of the highway that led me here,
a ribbon unfolding—it was so sure and blue, I knew
it would never do in anybody,
a moving place solid in the sunrise; concrete, surefooted.

I have not spoken for so long my words crack up,
they misfire and are not said after all.
Could you have imagined yourself here?
This is a whorehouse
where everyone comes, the ballistics of the highway,
a slow ascension into the immovable.

On one side or the other, despite our violent trajectory,
we could see the small plants, holding water
like a pension or a paycheck in their leaves,
in their intimacies.
Sleep avoids us; rum
like a primitive stone hammer

knocks us into a blank.

The boulders which embroider the edge of the sea
wink and nod under their constant bath,
fat attendants.
The thought slips from my hands, it has been slow.
At this point the highway ends, the desert
succeeds to its kingdom.

We're here to have fun.

I am not myself this morning; a tenant in army surplus.
The candy sand storms my head with a flat glitter
but she has a concentrated mind,
like Brooklyn.

Under the glassy lens of the Georgian Bay
I think there are germs, embryos,
and mossy, luminous fishes
that nobody owns.
With one finger a dead branch
juggles a sunrise moon.
I am followed by several people who say they are having fun.
They are laughing, they say.

The voice of dreams maintains that the world
will come to me
even though I am not sending out teams,
hacking my way through this world,
this jungle and impenetrable bush.
It does come: inch by stone,
leopard-spotted birds fall
out of the central heavens
with the noise of trip-hammers,
they plummet into the trefoil
with small and innocent crashes.
This all happens in the upper pasture.
From time to time
I become completely unimportant.
With immense relief I give up the creation
and re-creation of the entire world;
of course I could never make it work right
because of the details:
the oceans, species, manufacturing belts
around the major cities, and so on.
At this point someone comes up out of the red shift
and hands me a train ticket
to Laramie. I will have to speak
to the Cattlemen's Association
my unique message,
and I will take yours with me.
Write it down.
I promise to speak for both of us,
clear and unhindered as the dinner bell.
Ring me.

I want to desert you;
you have been terrible to me,
disregarding me, making me jealous.
If only you could be punished
and left on a highway somewhere;
you would be so ashamed of yourself
with nowhere to go.
No one would speak to you,
no one would take you in.

Women talk about people dying. We do this compulsively.
I have heard us everywhere, in Spanish Morocco,
Mexico, in Egremont Township, and the far
North. I have sampled all these strange tales.
People die in the most odd and terrible ways.
The only other people who talk like this are
policemen. Only they are more serious and
the stories are not second hand.

My mother reads a book about the San
Francisco earthquake and perforce she must
describe it to me: the fires, the bodies,
the collapsing walls which shoot out bricks
like cannonballs, beheading folks.
I have a collection of tales myself. There
are a couple I do not tell.

All women believe they are Scheherazade.
They believe they too will
or are about to die in burning buildings.
By telling these tales they divert.
It was other people all along.
Now maybe with the story
of the train wreck
you will leave me alone.
Did I say alone?
Let me restate that,
let me begin again.

This is Hill 49, an arena for bad dreams.
The wind is flaying this ridge to the bone,
peeling up membrane after membrane
of snow from the rocks.
A prismatic ring in the sky
wears the moon like a monocle.

I wonder what it's like under
that mild counterpane
where the low degrees that signify
      no heat
would agree with my metal lips and cheeks
that clang together
and betray me when I speak?

I am not a tone or note;
The creaks, the shrieks of alloys upon alloys
are my joints of knees and pelvis
moving in groups
the stiff, sequential troops of rivets.
I'm held up by an armature of nerves,
for which I take pills.
Mechanics come along and tender to my ills
with oilcans and greaseguns.
My eyes are red and full of thumbs.
This is sleep falling on me; snow.

And now, Dorothy, they are coming up the hill.
If, like a shotgun, I blew my brains out,
how many could we kill?
Tough luck for you, you pink thing,
all full of corpuscles and organs.
The shotgun hollers in a big balloon of sound

goodbye, goodbye.
I will settle
in the shadow of this dry rock
and be metal.

For hours you told me about you,
and people who loved you,
and those who said things about you
and what they said.

Late at night watching the animals
get up and turn over,
counting patches on the quilt,
listening to your voice
over the telephone
until the small hours.
When you were between men,
the bookends of your life.

Now there's another man,
a sort of male mother.
He will take care of things.
You wear him like a ring.
The calls have stopped,
and will not happen any more
until he leaves you.
Then the phone company
will rake in profits again;
this is what will happen,
take my word,
my best wishes,
everything but me for example.

I

A sentry is walking up and down singing a song in Spanish. He is a private in the Spanish Foreign Legion. He has got red tassels at both peaks of his cap. He has got red piping on his uniform. On his left arm under his sleeve he has a snake tattoo, it also has daggers. He's singing to keep himself awake. A song about a woman in Villafranca and how he walked up and down beneath her balcony in the rain. A strong sense of *forsakenness* often overcomes people in the Sahara.

Inside the sentry hut, the relief watch is making a fire on a shovel. Three cups, he says: one for life, one for love, and one for the next caravan out of Al Aaiún, which leaves only on Thursdays.

Al Aaiún means *the eye*. A spring is the eye of the desert. Interesting facts: "Every day the desert grows by forty square miles, and two hundred people die as a direct or indirect consequence."

Everybody waits all night in the sentry hut. At dawn the trucks will pull up; they're coming from Villa Cisneros loaded with tea, with cane sugar, with camel saddles, bales of blue cloth, figs with strange, white, threadlike worms in them, and goat cheese in salty hide containers. At 6:oo a.m. it will be very cold and the drivers will be smoking black tobacco, their sleeves pulled down over the five watches they wear on each arm. They are smuggling the watches into Morocco, and under each front seat there will be a lot of cassette recorders, same deal. They like smuggling things into Morocco. It's fun. The drivers appear to have glittering Rolex angel arms, they will be calling to each other: Did you see that whore last night in the cabaret?

2

At the edge of the oasis is a quonset hut; it is a cabaret for the Legion and the army officers. A thin, tired, clumsy Hassanayeen woman was dancing. On her layers of flimsy yellow-and-pink robes was a printed design which seemed to be composed of fish and roses.

"Mustafa" is a strange melody, somehow it is both fake and authentic, it is actually haunting. It's like necromancy—dead people are liable to show up to listen, smacking their lips. One thing about officers is that they always get paid. Earlier in the afternoon three of them in a jeep with machine guns picked up the photographer and went off somewhere with him. I waited for the sound of distant shots. How was I going to get out of the Sahara by myself? On reflection it appeared to be either impossible or dangerous. But they brought him back. They were just checking his papers. Sound of distant shots: rifle practice. They brought him back on Wednesday, and in the bar of the cabaret there were a lot of videogames with X-ray-blue lights that emitted the sounds of gunfire and accelerating machines. People like to check your papers. They like the *white sound* of papers and the photographs.

The sentry is walking up and down singing about Villafranca and the rain, about being under the bizarre black trees that make wet designs like fish bones in the rain. A man in a downpour, full of love or desire or simply a kind of emotional greed, this is what his song is about. *Mi amor.* About experience. Demonology, non-electronic.

Al Aaiún means *the eye.* Interesting facts: "Many persons who have had the experience of traveling across a desert report constant feelings of anxiety and forlornness during the journey. A feeling of having been *forsaken* overtakes one." There is only one bar in Al Aaiún, the officers' cabaret, and somebody plays "Mustafa" on a trumpet, and a tired, possibly hungry Hassanayeen woman takes off her clothes, revealing her body, which is a dark design of fish and roses. The Foreign Legionnaires have snake tattoos and pasts and debts. Some of them don't even watch her take off her clothes. Go sit in the sentry hut to wait for the caravan to form up and listen to the sentry sing about Villafranca in the rain, *mi amor, yo te quiero,* and so on, the rain, *la lluvia.*

Leaning against the wall of the sentry hut, I look at the relief watch making a pot of tea on the fire in the shovel, staring at the other life forms sitting around on the dirt floor. Against the other wall five Hassanayeen men in blue robes and black turbans are also observing; they seem like suspicious blue hallucinations or raptors. Their eyes move in fragmented sections, as if following the invisible movements of remote vehicles which only they can hear.

They have turned off the Arabic music coming through their transistor radios in order to listen to the sentry singing, in his frail Spanish voice, that if she doesn't lean out of the balcony only once and acknowledge him, standing under all that dangerous antique ironwork, in the rain, he'll go and join the Foreign Legion. He's lucky Spain still has a foreign legion. After they are thrown out of the Sahara they will have left only Al Hoceima, Ceuta, and Melilla. The sentry thinks, "I don't want to be transferred to Al Hoceima, there are centipedes up there as long as your socks, and at night they slowly march up your blankets, smacking their lips."

Outside, by herself, sits the woman who was dancing at the cabaret for the officers. Nobody talks to her. The men ask the photographer, What was my bride-price? He tells them a thousand English pounds. The relief watch makes tea on a shovel and I feel as if I am worth a thousand pounds English. Throw in a few goats. Take off one shoe and pour out the sand, take off the other shoe and pour out the sand, don't look anybody in the eye. *Mi amor, yo te quiero.*

3

Interesting facts: "The desert is expanding exponentially. The people who are the most affected are those who live on the fringes of the Sahara. Sandstorms occur with increasing frequency. The frightful famines that have visited Africa in recent years are only a ghastly prelude to a series of famines that will descend on humanity in the next several decades. Africa is a drying continent, over which the desert is continuing its inexorable advance."

Thursday continues its inexorable advance. The caravans are allowed to leave only on those mornings, to travel through an area mapped out in grids by the Spanish Army; hungry people are dangerous. A safe-conduct pass is issued to all foreign travelers; it has your photograph on it, taken with a flash, making you look as if you had been hit by lightning. Ancient fish bones make patterns in the rocks like Berber tattoos. Clouds are running up out of the Atlantic in long, dry lines, pure Sahara electronic clickings, digital clouds running right to left like Kufic script. The sentries handle their rifles carelessly, as if they were umbrellas. The brass rings that hold the webbing straps to the stocks glitter nervously in the firelight.

There are three cups, the sentry says: one for life, which is sweet; one for love, which is sweeter; and one for death, for after death is paradise and that is sweetest of all. Necromancy. Sand slithers in under the door like a sudden thought, creepy and pale.

At least, that's what the sentry claims the Arabs say, over their tea; he states this confidently and actually smiles as he hands the glasses around. The men in blue robes don't like to be told what Arabs say, especially by infidels; these are desert Arabs and what they know of European thought is the presence of soldiers, canned milk, alcohol, digital watches, Italian Western movies, and other filth. One of the men gets up, opens the door, and spits violently into the sand. Clouds are running up out of the west like shuttlecocks, white and dry. The dunes, too, are smooth, they lie without moving as shadows run across them in fugitive, demented dreams.

I get up and go outside. The sentries have loaded rifles and I have an odd feeling, as if I weighed a thousand pounds.

4

One of the men gets up, opens the door, and spits violently into the sand. "The desert is called *bahr bela ma,* sea without water." At five miles the curvature of the earth becomes apparent and things, short things, disappear below the horizon. There are the smaller dunes, called barkhans, which are migrating dunes shaped like a sickle. They often travel across the desert in lines more than sixty miles long. The drivers never know where to expect them; every Thursday they have changed, because the dunes migrate on Wednesdays as well. The drivers run around the edges of the barkhans, trying to stay on the hammada, a gravelly, stony floor of fragmenting pebbles. "Then there are the great star dunes, which can reach a thousand feet and do not move; they can serve for many years as landmarks." It has been five years since it rained. The desert is expanding exponentially.

At five miles the curvature of the earth intervenes, and when we leave at dawn we and all the other short things will disappear below the sentries' horizon. Arabic music in the background gives an intense, sinister feeling to these occurrences. It is just before dawn. Everything the moon says is true. Ramadan migrates through the

76

calendar, the month of hunger. Outside the military perimeter, the beautiful dunes have no color and migrate in long lines like free traders bringing famine. Don't like that, do you? says the sentry to the man who went outside to spit. That's what you people say, isn't it? Death is sweetest of all?

All this is going on in Spanish and I get up and go outside. The photographer doesn't understand Spanish, but I don't warn him. I hardly know him. He's come up all the way from Mauritania; he keeps his eyes on the steam from the glass of tea. I can't tell you how cold it is. Stars stare straight down through the atmosphere, curious and alien. In the cabaret the soldiers are putting fifty-peseta coins in the videogames; one of these games appears to be a caravan of eight trucks running across the hammada, which you, the pilot, try to catch in a crossfire.

5

The woman who took her clothes off and has Berber fish-bone tattoos on her chin is leaning against the outside wall of the sentry hut, because the men won't let her come in. She's a whore. She's playing with a digital watch with the sweet, pleased fascination of a small child. She has looked in the window of the hut and has seen the brass armbands the men are wearing. Maybe that's why she's outside. Inside the windings of the brass wire little pieces of paper are tucked in; there are certain verses from the Koran written on these papers and these special verses have the magical property of protecting the wearer from bullets. Sorcery, very freaky. This means after they take the caravan into the desert on Thursday they assume they are going to be shot at, at least by Friday. By whom is an interesting question. Don't ask, don't look at the wrong people, we will be in Morocco by a week from Sunday. The woman is very dirty and very thin. One of the men comes outside and spits violently into the sand.

Then I come out. This is the way it works: Only saints and bandits know how unimportant is the human body. Include soldiers. The pair is the smallest unit in which the more highly developed life forms can endure cosmic dimensions, and what you have here—the

Sahara, the famine, the war—is cosmic dimensions. I sit down beside the woman and hand her a tin of sardines. She jams it instantly into her robes.

Riding on top of the load of sugar and tea and bales of blue cloth tomorrow I will look up into the sky, and you know what? We are hanging upside down on the bottom of the planet, staring with intrepid unconcern into outer space. I will be overcome by a feeling both passive and suicidal, you want to jump. The dancer/whore will have pulled her seven veils over her head against the tearing wind. A sudden, soundless avalanche of sand occurs on a distant cliff face; the whole face falls off. Cosmic. As a child, I used to try to love God but at the same time I was afraid He would lean down out of heaven and take a bite out of my head. *Allah,* says the man who came outside. He goes back in and sits down. Famine has become normal and the other thing is that I hardly know the photographer and I wonder if he's planning on going off on his own when we reach Tantan. The sentry's song makes it sound as if he were soaked and dripping, drowning in a downpour in a little Iberian square in Villafranca. The woman who took off her clothes in the cabaret plays with a kind of beeper on her digital watch, listening to it intently. The sun is about to come up. Everything the sun says is true, and it is referred to as "she" in Arabic. We are at the perimeter, and back in the white, rounded domes of the oasis town, you can see the old fort, radio aerials rising like fish bones.

6

There are places in the Sahara where only microorganisms can exist. I find this interesting but strange, and actually frightful. Ahead of us it is four hundred miles to the nearest water. The photographer says in Tantan they sell it by the cup, one for day and one for night and one for the curvature of the earth, where at five miles you disappear below the horizon with all the other short things that are either short naturally or short because they are collapsing and can no longer stand. At the next plateau we pass tomorrow, an entire cliff face will disappear. All across the peach-colored dunes *miradores* like lighthouses stand up; they are watching the expanding and dangerous desert with rectangular green eyes, which are radar, and the little radar screens make faint crackling noises as we move across them, green dots on time and on Thursday, with all our passes in order. Arabic music forms an intense, sinister background, the volume turned up. In the middle of the desert people draw together, a sense of having been *forsaken* manifests itself. The sky has become lower at dawn; little spongy gray clouds tear past at eight thousand feet, running right to left like Arabic script. At this point I am absolutely unacquainted with anybody else's body, not the outside body, but the inside body, which is a great star dune, the color of a peach, solid and immutable. It's just a matter of staying close to the photographer, his body is a windbreak. Yesterday he got taken away by several men with machine guns in a jeep and I ran after him down the narrow, blazing streets; the fear of being *forsaken* overtakes people in the hammada. In a small room in Tantan, in the inn, the fonduk, I will look up and see the photographer watching me in the mirror. All the other short things will have disappeared below the curvature of the pure Sahara with its electronic clickings, a vast videogame we are programmed to lose, and the woman dancer with the fishbone Berber tattooing on her chin is a kind of demented singular unit; she and her robes printed with fish and roses will disappear into the streets of Tantan, keeping on toward Morocco, where people are not so hungry. Famine is a state of absence, but the desert is growing exponentially, filling up the hungry places and the sickle-shaped barkhans the way free traders offer their soft yellow wares from oasis to oasis, from Villa Cisneros, to Al Aaiún, to Tantan and Sidi Ifni, and are reaching up to Béni Mellal.

As a city, Tantan is almost totally yellow.

7

Interesting facts: "One incident will serve to demonstrate how powerful the grinding action of sand can be. After forty-eight hours of a hurricane-force sandstorm, the glass in all the vehicles had become opaque from the sandblasting and the windshields had to be knocked out before the journey could continue."

In the middle of the journey everything we are carrying will assume enormous importance, the cameras, the dried figs, the tin of sardines, the goat cheese. The water bags, made of goatskin, shaped like goats. I will look back and see our tracks running backward toward Al Aaiún, proof that we have a past, and a future, where I will make more tracks. The tracks go back through time to the Islands, Europe, North America, and assure me I must have had a beginning.

We will pass a man whose three camels are lying in the stony gravel of the hammada, perhaps dead. We will pass him at sixty miles an hour. The melody of "Mustafa" forms a manic background to the caravan's race from Al Aaiún to water, and every minute we are seduced in the arms of the barkhans, their silken, slippery sands, and throw down the sand tracks and dig out again and again, is several more pints of water lost. The body is a water clock. Planes will pass by overhead, very low, violent archangels with snake tattoos. Enfamined people are listening to pointless songs on electronic devices, and people who are hungry are often dangerous, or dying. The actual physical body of the photographer assumes enormous importance and assures me I must have a presence. He leans against the whitewashed wall of the room in the fonduk, and when I look up from the water basin, I will see him watching me in the mirror. Listen to what I'm telling you. Sidi Ifni is now almost completely deserted.

The trucks are gunning their motors, a bright avalanche prepared to accelerate into the Sahara. We climb up the slats of the sides; they are big red Mercedes, hot as forges. The dawn wind tears sideways through our loose clothing. Throw in everything, jump in after, the soldiers are coming around and I hold out my safe-conduct, which rattles and tears. The death rate is growing by almost two hundred people a day and short things keep disappearing below the curvature of the earth. We shoot forward into the Sahara, I have fallen back upon hard times and cane sugar, the Berber dancer bursts out laughing, spongy gray clouds run up on this Thursday out of the Atlantic, and for ten shocking minutes, rain falls.

ZERELDA

I

She, like all the best people,
came from Kentucky; she is on
her third husband and has never been
happy since the first one died in
California, preaching the Word
of God or maybe he was
panning gold himself, who knows? A Reverend Robert
    James,
sick and biblical, passed away on
    the 22nd inst. of this year 1850
    with his penultimate breath said
    I am far from Zerelda and my boys, God keep
    them
et cetera and then shuffled off this mortal coil
(which appears to be a sort of clay snake)
having never in his life
entered a bar or tavern,
sworn out loud, read salacious literature, or
fired a shot in anger.

II

Here are her sons, Jesse and Frank,
small consolation prizes out of the goldfields;
they are her own, at least so far.
She can neither vote nor sit on a jury
nor go around without the ironclad corsets
or speak aloud of anything she knows to be true;
she is alive and yet without

a legal existence.
The law does not allow her husband to beat her
with a cane any thicker than his thumb.
So she will get another husband
who is smaller, whose thumbs
are not so big.

III

Big emotions sweep over Zerelda,
tornadoes and electrical storms; the Civil War
was made for people like Zerelda;
she does not even resist but sails off
like a barn roof.
    They are simple emotions: rage, fear,
    a desire to be noticed.
In her mouth human speech becomes a skinning
    knife:
They're going to take our niggers away,
they think they're better than we are,
    and so on.
She expands into a rage at the mill:
she thinks she's been cheated, she goes after
George William Liddle with a potato spade.
    (Can you imagine Zerelda dancing, can you
    imagine Zerelda seventeen years old and
    dancing in Kentucky?)

IV

At the end of the line of wagons at the mill there
is a black woman with two sacks of field corn and a

jar of zinnias. She is taking the zinnias to her
    mother
if she can. The woman sees the conflict coming and
    backs
the mules. "Sshh-back, sshh-back" and the zinnias
    nod
with accurate brown centers. She has to get the
    field
corn ground into kitchen meal and back home and
    now
look what's going on. The woman is owned by a
    man
named Billy Garshade who lives at Cracker Neck.
COLORED RECRUITS! $100 BOUNTY
AND PAY NOT EXCEEDING
$300 TO LOYAL OWNERS! She can easily
imagine herself
dancing. The mules back up against the singletree
and the trace chains crash with a noise like water
or hope.

V

The boys don't like to see their mother cheated,
they believe her, they have always believed her
            and now it is Civil War.
Down the road comes a troop of local Union militia
in blue uniforms;
leading them is George William Liddle.

VI

Frank has already joined the guerrillas.
Jesse is fifteen and plowing in the fields
when the militia rides in, they shut
Zerelda up like the whole neighborhood
secretly wished somebody would shut
her up, with a rifle butt.
They find Jesse at the plow and beat him half
to death with the reins.
This is called Civil War.
Enormous thoughts or desires crash and
collide with each other, theories, ideologies.
Zerelda is screaming, of course; they
will finally burn her out under
General Order Number 11.

> (Can you imagine Zerelda dancing? Can you
> imagine Zerelda seventeen years old and
> dancing in Kentucky?)

VII

As the years go by Zerelda gets more dramatic.
Oh, Mother, say the huge famous bandits.
They are sick of problems with no solution.
Look up from your soap-making, Zerelda, stop
        muttering
to yourself, possessed by rages, cheated, vengeful,
thinking you are in actuality making soap.
Stop talking to yourself.
The larger questions of life are for you as well
down the ladder of summer cumulus, out of the
arctic of noon, out of the cosmic laundry of
gigantic clouds comes either death or eternal life.

Detectives throw a bomb in the window.
Archie is killed, Zerelda's hand is blown off.
Oh, Mother.
    (Can you imagine Zerelda dancing?)

VIII

Zerelda learns to make soap, wash clothes,
    clean the lamp chimneys, shovel the ashes
from the fireplace with one hand;
    the other is a steel hook.
Does she seem like a monster-woman from
    folktales or legends?
She is,
she didn't get this way by herself,
she had help.

FRANK INVITES JESSE TO JOIN HIM IN
QUANTRELL'S GUERRILLAS: SEPTEMBER 1862

I am coming back for you, leave the house after
    supper,
meet me at Low Gap, I will come with two horses,
    one in each
hand, they will be striped with darkness and the
    shadow
of deep wells.

We will move like clocks through the night hours.
    We will work
for ourselves and when we like we will be
    unemployed as the

goldenrod and the grass. It is better than owning
      things, it is
better even than getting elected.

Meet me at Low Gap. I will give you a horse of
      violence and
delight, I will give you a horse of agency and black
      powder.
The world is different than we used to think,
      houses catch fire
more easily than they said, killing is simple,
      dynamite is
also fast. The world around us is made of
      matchsticks and
rye straw.
I am telling you, reality is unstable.

Sit on the rails by the salt spring tonight, I will see
      your
cigarette, wait for me at Low Gap, under the broad
      shoulder
of Rattlesnake Hill, stars spark in the dark roach of
      its
diamond back.

We will not be officially counted and no one will
      have time
to call us by our names.

Only saints and killers know firsthand
the red fragility of the human body,
the low gear-ratio of the human mind.

There were bands of robbers moving continually through [Cooper] county, who cared nothing for either party, who robbed and killed without discrimination or regard to party. During the year 1864 many good citizens belonging to either side were shot down, first by one side and then by the other, and many citizens abandoned their homes, seeking places of more security. The details of these murders and robberies are too disgraceful and sickening to enumerate in this brief history.

The History of Cooper County
Steam Book Job Printers, St. Louis, 1879

GUERRILLA WARFARE: MISSOURI 1856–1865

I

It is a war we have invented to our own liking.
It is homemade, off-the-wall,
we have invented many new ideas in our war
with our neighbors;
the new ideas are:
bushwhacking
leading Quakers into ambushes
killing all the men over the age of twelve in any
particular town
(Lawrence, Osceola, Danville, Poplar Bluff)
and throwing people down wells.
Anyway, they are new to us.

Altogether, we make something bigger than one
    alone,

more explosive, a group of men reaching
critical mass.
We are the atoms of an unstable substance, moving
    toward
fission,
we suddenly fuse and go off.

II

The unarmed federals leaping out of the cattle cars
in Centralia yell stop or something.
Our rifle barrels are hot as pokers
we can't stop ourselves
we are being run by something
that lives in us as if we were an abandoned house.
It is watching and watching out of our eyeholes.

*I don't know what it is or what it wants, but I can tell you
this:
we don't come natural to it.*

III

Frank's house is not abandoned,
after all the killing and escapes he
lays up in a corncrib west of Rocheport
reading the constitutional theories of Robert
    Ingersoll,
fingerprints of grease and black powder marking
    the
hot-lead print.
Bloody Bill and Charlie and Fletcher Taylor are
    suspicious;

they eat their sidemeat and fried mush watching
    him,
they know the only thing
looking out of Frank's eyeholes is Frank.
Leave him alone, says Jesse. *You just have to leave him*
    read.

COLUMBIA MISSOURI STATESMAN: SEPTEMBER 27, 1864

Included here is a list of the members of Company A, 39th Reg-
iment of Missouri Volunteers, lost near Centralia by Anderson's Bush-
whackers.

This is a correct list of all lost and missing. There may be such
a thing that one or two may come in, but nearly every man was found
and recognized on the field and scattered in the neighborhood within
a few miles, some as far off as six miles from Centralia.

PENNY DREADFUL

Read here how the Missouri Guerrillas rode
    through storms of shot (how does
it go?) and anyway, the killing, you'll love it.
    Bloody Bill Anderson is not very efficient as
    guerrillas go but
he alone is worth the price of admission.
    Read how he rides in to the attack weeping and
    foaming at the mouth
after the federals killed his sisters in a Kansas City
    prison (they didn't
mean to, it was mainly that the building collapsed
    but to hear B.B. tell
it), tears rush down his face as he screams and fires,

his mother
throws her apron over her head and sobs,
When will it all end?
What do you mean, end? We just got started.
Fletcher Taylor does heroics, Charlie Pitts starts
fires, and
Frank, reserved as usual, takes time out for a good
cigar.
Jesse is hard to see
he survives
he is sixteen, he knows already to stay very
quiet and
aim for the middle.
He operates like an empty space, he shifts.
Around him are atmospheres while in the
foreground
more heroics; a cover story.

THE END OF THE WAR: RETURNING FROM
AN ATTEMPTED SURRENDER: JUNE 1865

This is the story of how it all started. Of how none
of this was our
fault. We are trying to get home, telling ourselves
this story.

We are taking the long way around, Jesse's chest
wound leaks down his
shirt, it makes his belt sticky, at night we have to
pour hot water

into his boots before we can get them off, he is
soaked in fluids,

blood, and plasma, we only had one frying pan and
    Charlie Pitts

lost that. Jesse was riding into Burns's Schoolhouse
    with his hands
in the air, calling out he was coming in to
    surrender. We may be

guerrillas but we knew the etiquette, you're
    supposed to hand in
your sword or something and say, Thank you for
    the lovely war,

we'll do the same for you next time, and they fired.
    The first shot
took off half his middle finger, left hand, the
    second shot got

him in the chest and he went flying backwards out
    of the saddle
and took the bedroll with him. It was him and
    Fletcher Taylor.

Fletcher went back to get him. We laid up for a
    week in a triangular
hogpen somebody had knocked together in the
    corner of a rail fence.

Jesse said he's had it up to here with surrendering,
    if he keeps it
up it'll be the death of him. Then it was a matter of
    getting him

back across the Missouri River, riding on the

strange sliding action
of the flooding water which was like a long material
      being drawn and

drawn underneath the ferry, the far shore coming
      at us in the night
with a slow, expanding movement. We walked past
      the detachment

of federals on the other side like visiting angels on
      our way to
some other annunciation. Jesse said it made him
      feel shameful

and incontinent to be breathing in two places at
      once and in front
of strangers. Charlie wakes us up too early in the
      mornings, he

has either nightmares or visions, he said he saw this
      giant
guinea hen in the oaks two mornings ago, skulking
      there with

its head bowed, quoting text from Leviticus. "It was
mournful," he said, "and fearsome." The worst
      thing about Pitts

is that somebody taught him to play the juice harp.
      Jesse rides
upright now, the wound is shutting itself like a
      bank vault

over his safe and valuable heart, nobody notices the

rare skeletons
of birds or the sudden hair of milkweed, our pods
    are not broken,

the soul does not float on the octaves of the wind,
    all the wars
and reasons for wars are lost, but we will make up
    our own

reasons. We will make up our own story. At
    Appomattox the federal
government learned its fatal lesson; that anything
    can be solved

by the application of superior force. This is what
    happens to
winners. They begin to believe in winning.

And now the federal government believes in banks.
So do we.
We believe in banks.

JESSE MEETS HIS FUTURE WIFE, ZEE MIMMS

Here she is coming in with medicines, with
    bandages for
his infected life.
She can see everything in this big hole in his
    thoughts.
She can see the faulty reason beating and beating,
the lost causes,
the parts that are missing, the blood and the lungs.

There are things that live inside of wounds;
a certain memory fixed in his body forever,
a hole in the heart of Dixie, just south of his
    breastbone.
It was the last time he ever exposed his heart.
It was the last time he ever put his hands
above his head
except for her.

Every man is owed a wife; wives live in a different
    country,
a country of women without civil wars, or trains, or
    motivations.
They arrive with bandages; he imagines they never
    surrender
except to him.

She will make a design of his life, a quilt pattern
rusty with blood, made up of the rags
of women's dresses.
Log Cabin, Courthouse Steps, the Road to
    California.

He says: Marry me.
He says: I want to be able to stop,
just stop and watch you,
a hawk pouring out of the long prairie air
carrying between your wings a commission from the
    fertile sun
and your soul, which will have to serve for us both
and move through us both
like a wind through the bottom fields

an invisible comb, I will be moved and marked
and finally harvested.
Why don't you marry me, he says. Tend to all these
wars, and the broken thoughts, and the open
     wounds.

THE KILLING OF JOHN W. SHEETS: GALLATIN, MISSOURI, 1865

This is a stick-up:
your money or your life.
We are beginning to understand they will always
     choose the money
but a force has been filling Jesse for days, he is
     under
pressure or water,
he turns at the door of the bank and you could see
his whole soul and the entire static charge pour out
not once but five times.
The Gallatin Farmer's Bank crashed with the noise—
flashes, bangs, hot blue surprises.
Life flies out of the man with his hands up
like the air from a balloon.
Jesse's blaze-faced sorrel horse bolts and drags him
down the main street of Gallatin
banging his head off the town pump.
I pulled him up behind, my horse sank and lunged
carrying two grown men and a sack of dollars,
two heavy men and a sack full of money.
He said he thought he was going to get blown away
but it was kind of an exciting feeling.

Frank's trial
by General Jamin Matchett

I lived three miles from Winston at the time of the robbery. Believe I saw Frank James at my residence on July 14, 1881. A Mr. Scott was with him. One of the party rode a bay, the other a sorrel with two white hind legs. I came downstairs to the front door. They wanted to know if they could get dinner. I said I would see my wife, who objected somewhat, as she was washing, to which they remarked they were in no hurry, and I then told them they could be accommodated. When they rode up I noticed they were wearing heavy goods for that time of year and had gum coats or blankets strapped to the saddles. The defendant said his name was Willard . . . and came from the Shenandoah Valley. I inquired of Willard where he had been between the Shenandoah Valley and this section, and never answered me, but said, "What do you think of Bob Ingersoll?" We discussed Bob for some time, till we differed, so that I went to my library for a volume of his lectures, and he read some till he fell asleep. [After dinner]: Willard wanted to pay for the dinner, and I declined at first, but finally took fifty cents. In conversation with Scott he observed he would take me for a minister of the Christian Church, and I answered that I was. He said he thought if he ever united with the church he would join the Christian Church and referred to his wife as a Presbyterian. Willard acquiesced in that, but said there was no man ever lived like Shakespeare, and declaimed a piece and remarked, "That's grand!" which observation I endorsed. Finally Scott said something about going and I invited them, if they ever came that way, to call again, which they said they would be pleased to do, that they were going to Gallatin, where Willard said he had not been for ten years.

Cross-examined: I am this confident the defendant is the man who stopped at my house that if he hadn't paid for the dinner I would say, "Mr. Willard, I would be pleased to have the amount of that board bill." [*Laughter*]

After a while they get good at it,
it becomes easy and practiced;
like anybody who does the same trick over and over
     they
get bored.

Charlie is still setting fires, playing
the juice harp, Fletcher went to Oklahoma
a long time ago, the Youngers argue with
each other about land or general principles,
Frank wants to go somewhere and farm.

Jesse keeps them at it, the only solution
for the boredom is to make mistakes once
in a while, or get married, or rob
something more complicated.
So he does all three.
One of these solutions is fatal.

It was back when the art was still primitive:
     they used cap-and-ball
     getaway horses
     everything was slow motion and
four-four time,
     a ballad in fact, with end-stopped lines
predictable
     nothing could move faster than a running horse
except trains, the telegraph, or
     the human mind.

Maybe the human mind is not as fast
as we thought.

Western Union Telegraph Company, Jefferson City,
  Missouri, December 24,
1869. Rec'd at Independence, Missouri, Attention
  Sheriff of Clay County.

You will at once organize, arm and equip as militia
  thirty or more men and
aid Tomlinson Deputy Sheriff of Clay County if
  called on in capturing
or killing Frank James and Jesse James or hold such
  force in readiness
to aid you in such capture or killing if they be
  found in your county.
The state will pay expense of force for actual
  service and five hundred
(500) dollars for capture and killing of each. I write
  by mail. J. W. McClurg

WANTED POSTER

Jesse Woodson James: five feet eleven inches tall, brown hair, regulation killer-blue eyes. In photographs appears to be considering shooting the photographer. Does not test out well. Approaches casual strangers in an intimate way and interferes massively in their private lives. Is trapped in the dead hole and neither moves nor changes. Steals horses. Inhabits a discolored landscape through which only one, treacherous path is known to pass. Has the appearance of many ballistics with a flat trajectory. This man is occupied by an army of scars, tip of middle finger left hand missing, and one large scar on chest which oft has spoken with bloody lips. Is always breaking out afresh. Cultivates a desperado aura and can most often be seen in the penny dreadfuls, spotted regularly in novels, poems, ballads, and folktales. Men claiming to be James can be differentiated from him in that they pose willingly in front of cameras, they make political speeches. These people are not the genuine article and are confused. Jesse James was never confused about anything in his life, which will last exactly thirty-seven years, five months, three days, fourteen hours, and ten minutes.

ESCAPES

The front end of the horse is the suspension,
the back end is the drive;
in sudden plunges down shaly slopes your
heels are jammed down, the Achilles tendon
taut as a bowstring, providing forward impetus, and if
you come to a sudden halt caused by things such as
bullets or fence rails you
will be shot from the saddle like a bolt from a
crossbow, you
will decorate trees—that white oak there, for
instance, they call them hanging trees.

The detectives who are not far behind in
geospace or relative time on this
train of thought will crowd up on
their present tense, they will
fire at will, they will
look into each other's eyes, it will
be a kind of true love,
        they will all shoot each other.

Or maybe they will try to turn him like spies or
informers are turned. We need a man like you, Jesse,

and have been looking for somebody of your caliber
to give out our press releases
    a kind of cosmic postman
America's Candygram, a Western Union
of all our underground intentions,
our hard copy whose statement is this:
bang.

Sitting up all night in Dick Liddle's
dirty whorehouse near Richmond by lantern
light he's filing down some metal piece and
    clearing his throat, he's waiting
for them,
    he is either crazy or so self-contained that
there is no room for anything else but him-
    self and that's no heroics, it's just the simple
single-mindedness of rattlesnakes.
    A bullet stops the detective's horse,
the detective emerges from a hard run into a
    treetop.
    There's something I've been meaning to tell you
    and
that is, I don't like it when you come up
    behind me like that.

BANDITS' WIVES

What Zee is doing all these years is a mystery, or
    maybe not so
much mysterious as ignored;
    no different from any other housewife in the
    nineteenth century,

in Missouri
    she has to balance everything carefully, how to
    make Jesse the
center of her life but yet not become too
    dependent; after all, her
husband's work takes him away from home all the
    time, she has to make
some decisions by herself
    but then on the other hand she can't get too
    independent. Jesse
likes to be the head of the household, you know
    how it is, the money
she spends is not her own, it's not Jesse's either but
    let that go
for now.
    Can you imagine being engaged to a bank
    robber for seven years and
he's your first cousin besides; the marriage was
    fairly quiet.
    Oh, well, it's all in the family and those Missouri
    rural clans are
tight.
    Zee never wanted to end up like Belle Starr or
    Cattle Kate or
Poke Alice. Those violent whores are attractive to
    historians but
they are usually diseased or dead after a while, the
    whores I mean,
and besides it's no fun having people spit on your
    skirt.
    Zee is a good Missouri girl from the right
    background.
    Her life and that of Frank's wife Annie is the
    kind of life you

have to imagine or invent, such as the time
    the chimney fire nearly burnt the house down
    and Zerelda said
you have to pour salt down the chimney! and sent
    Annie up on the roof
with a washpan full of salt and Annie's petticoat
    lace caught on a
nail and it all tore off in a strip and nobody noticed
    it till later.
Frank saw this strip of lace hanging from the roof
    gutter like a celebration,
    yes, everybody laughed about it for years. And
    the time
    Frank taught Annie to play poker and so Annie
    went over to Zee's
house with a pack of cards and taught her, and
    then Zerelda caught them
playing at gambling and said what the hell are the
    people at the New
Hope Baptist Church going to think about this? so
    Zee hid the cards
in one of Jesse's socks and Jesse never did figure
    out where they came
from. And the time
    Zerelda borrowed Annie's little portable sewing
    machine and never
gave it back no matter how many times Annie asked
    her for it, and one
night Frank came in and said, *We've got to go to*
    Tennessee, right now,
get the kids ready, they'd done another bank robbery
    or something,
so Annie and Zee went over in the middle of the
    night and got the

sewing machine and hid it in the wagon so they
       were halfway to Jefferson
City before Zerelda even knew it was gone. When
       they were going along
in the wagon Annie said, "Well, I guess now I'm as
       big a robber as you
are, Frank, ha ha ha," and Frank didn't know what
       the hell to make of
that. And the time
       Jesse and two of the gang were at home doing
       as little as possible
and Zee said she was feeling like homemade sin
       with this cold. "Jesse,
give me a hand with the house, would you?" and
       he did; you talk about
a desperate outlaw doing the dishes, wearing that
       Navy Colt five-shot
revolver, standing at the sink, soap bubbles caught
       in the blond hair
of his forearms, singing "I'm a Good Old Rebel"
       and he said, "Honey, I'll
get the sitting room," and he lifted both hands
       above his head to straighten
a picture of Dan Patch whereupon Robert Ford
       shot him in the back of the head twice
at close range.

JESSE IS THROWN OUT OF THE
NEW HOPE BAPTIST CHURCH

(Founding Preacher, Reverend Robert James)

Minutes of the New Hope Baptist Church
Kearney, Missouri
August 12, 1876

The covenant of the New Hope Baptist Church
was called for and read.
A motion that the church get seven spittoons
for the use of the
congregation.
Carried.
It was requested Sister Dixie Thompson be
excluded from the church;
she being found guilty of dancing. Moved that the
hand of fellowship
be withdrawn.
Carried.
Brother Elias Halloway confessed to having
made a false impression
and requested forgiveness. He having made suitable
amends, the question
was considered.
Forgiveness voted.
The case of Brother Jesse Woodson James
being considered, charges
of revelry, robbery, murder, intemperance, and
other un-Christian acts
being preferred, and he manifesting an impenitent
spirit, motion that
the hand of fellowship be withdrawn and he be
excluded from the church.
Carried.

On motion of Brother Hancock, Sister
    Georgina Williams to be excluded
from the fellowship of the church upon charges of
    walking disorderly
and having run off to join the Campbellites.
    Carried.
    After sermon by pastor, the doors of the church
    were opened to
membership. None responded.

Clerk: Jno Burnett

FOLK TALE

One day Frank and Jesse and Bob and Cole were
    riding down the road
to home with saddlebags full of gold. And they
    came on a farm where a
woman was out doing her washing in the yard. They were
    all hungry so they
stopped and said,
    Say, ma'am, would you cook us some dinner,
    we are real hungry.
    (They didn't have any restaurants in those days,
    my mother explains.)
    And the woman said,
    Hell no, can't you tell a person's doing a
    laundry when you see it?
    But, ma'am, we are real hungry, and we will
    pay you for it.
    No, I ain't going to do it, she said.
    But look here, you could cook us a chicken, I
    see you got a lot of

chickens there and I'll even kill one for you.
    And he whipt out his pistol and shot the head
    off a chicken.
    Well now, since you done kilt that chicken you
    can just gut it and
pluck it, she said. She was so mad she was hopping
    around the yard, lookt
like somebody killing snakes with a switch.
    And all the boys razzed Jesse and laught at him
    and shoved him off
his horse and he had to sit down and gut and pluck
    that chicken. And she
went and fried it for them and charged them a high
    enough price for it,
I can tell you. And the boys never let him live it
    down, when they would
be riding hard away from the law and they saw
    some chickens somebody would
yell
    Oh, Jesse, I want my dinner, go shoot me that
    chicken. Oh, Jesse, we're
hungry, blow the head off that rooster, will you?
    There are good days and bad days in the life of
    a bank robber. My
mother swears this story is true. The farmer's wife
    was trying to teach
them that you have to eat what you kill.
    Think of yourself as a chicken.

Trial of Frank James: Testimony: Clarence Hite's Confession

Jesse killed Ed Miller. He killed him in Jackson or Lafayette counties last spring was a year ago. They were in a fuss about stopping to get some tobacco, and after riding some distance, Ed shot at Jesse and shot a hole through his hat and then Jesse turned and shot him off his horse. The watch I got out of the Blue Cut robbery is at home. Just before I was arrested I hid it between the bed ticks. Frank gave the jewelry to his wife he got out of the Blue Cut robbery. Jesse said last summer if he only knew on what train Governor Crittenden was he would take him off and hold him for a ransom—thought he could get about $25,000.

CONFESSIONS OF GANG MEMBER CHARLIE PITTS, KILLED AT NORTHFIELD, SEPTEMBER 7, 1876

I rode into Northfield, Minnesota, with voices in my head telling me forget it, it's not worth it, but I stopped listening to them ever since these voices I mentioned told me to eat axle grease for my sins when I was ten and I ate it and was damn sorry. Nothing east of Hundred and Two Mile River except big dead chickens and rusty pig snouters nowadays. Upside my head is a strawberry mark big as a dollar. This means I have good luck and foresight and get flashes of things that come up out of the back of my head. Listen to the happy pistols clicking and saying their piece. Nothing makes Jesse so content as shooting people. We got other people living inside us, just under the skin, these inside people are not male nor are they female, they are kind of purple-black like the skins of Spanish onions, and they have the same pearly shine. Last night mine begun to slide out of me through the hole in the top of my head through which so much else has escaped too, when I was looking after my horse Sweet Pea, she had a great big locust thorn stuck in her gums. This onion creature began to get fed on the lantern light and slide out of my person. I would have been struck blind and dumb, I would have went and eat axle grease again. This is the thing makes everybody kill people.

Here we go up to Northfield now, this is us getting close to Northfield. We're going to die here and get shot up until we look like sieves. They're gonna run us into a swamp and yell, Surrender, and one of the Youngers is gonna yell back, We don't surrender much, and it will get writ in a book. I'll never get to tell anybody or any one person what it is makes us kill people. Whatever we get in life is provisional. It will eat you in sections and you will die all at once. This thing has been talking out of my mouth all my life and now I will be hit in that selfsame mouth. People who have messages are struck dumb and folks who don't have a damn thing to talk about never shut up. Oh, God, how I loved shooting people. Me and my onion woulda blown up whole cities if I'da had the gunpowder. I will finally win the argument with the purple-black party inside, which was flying out toward the simple lantern in the barn and Sweet Pea and the world. Leaving me to voices and rye straw. This is Northfield, my Minnesota onion war.

POCKETS

In the pockets of the corpse of Bill Chadwell, killed
    at Northfield,
there was found a map of the Western states, a
    pocket compass, a box
of salve, a Howards gold watch, an article on the
    Yale lock torn from the
local paper, gold sleeve buttons with enameled
    leaves, and a gold ring.

In the pockets of Clell Miller, killed at Northfield,

there was found
a gold Waltham watch, ten cents, an advertisement
   for a Halt's safe with
an engraving depicting a robber giving up on trying
   to enter it, and a
business card from a St. Peters, Minnesota, livery
   stable.

In the pockets of Charlie Pitts, alias Samuel Wells,
   there was found
five cents, a label from a whiskey bottle, and a
   Spanish onion.

FRANK GETS NERVOUS ABOUT JESSE'S KILLER INSTINCTS

You grow blue in the steamy days of July, the
   depths of heat in your
shrunken house in St. Jo, blind shadows.

I hear cries, shouts, the final appeals of men
   working out some
predictable destiny in a swamp, out of ammunition,
   crude as ore.
These sounds appear to come from my dreams.

Sometimes you are there, soaked in oak shadows,
   the hard shells of
mental ammunition, green shade moving like
   suspicious neighbors where
next door is always full of armed men, the very
   guinea hens call your
name as if it were the announcement of a fabulous
   act, the very yard

dogs appear quiet and stiff with intent as
        undertakers, nobody pities
your hard, red karma.

This is what was made of you, stuffed into a
        five-button cutaway suit,
the fingers into gloves, arms into the linen shells of
        drover's dusters;
we see you coming a mile off, riding right through
        Clay County and into
folklore, clashing with real federal silver dollars,
        realer than we
have seen in a long, long time.

Through the blackberry and sumac east of
        Otterville, at Rocky Cut,
you get the drop on everybody. Talk about trains.
        It was so daring
and so daylight.

It was too bad about Northfield. If only you had
        asked the right people.
But all along the turnpike behind, here comes our
        long company: Captain
John W. Sheets, D. W. Griffith, Joseph Lee
        Haywood, Frank Wymore, Frank
McMillan, the unarmed federals we were shooting
        three at a time at
Centralia.

What I will answer for is not the federals or the
        bank clerks but that I
came back for you at Low Gap, full of persuasion
        and leading horses.

I cocked you like a pistol, you were efficient and
      fifteen. "And I
said: Oh, that I had wings like a dove! For I would
      fly away and be at
rest. Lo, I would flee far away and live in the
      wilderness." Psalm 55.

The young men who are joining us now are
      treacherous and don't remember
the war. Something moves and grows in me like an
      apology, a hope, a
mass demonstration. At night when I sleep my
      hands fall each to one side
empty as clothes without people in them. I think
      this is how husbands
are, in their own beds, in their own time.

RAISING HOGS

September of 1876 Frank rides quietly away from
      Northfield
toward Tennessee like the whole thing was just
      embarrassing;
it was hardly human, he won't let Jesse drag him
      into
these things again.
Frank's going to Tennessee and raise hogs.
He crosses the river at Cape Girardeau.
It's a very hot river town, the Mississippi is actually
      hot,
it's steaming, nobody asks who you are.
He is seduced by all the simple normal people at
      the

ferry landing, he will send for Annie and the kids,
he is crossing the river into Little Egypt,
he's going into agriculture as if it were a religion,
the Holy Fire Church of Prophecy and Pigs.
There will be peace in Waverly County,
they have relatives down there they can count on,
never go anyplace you don't have relatives.
It's all in how a man comports himself
walking upright amongst the swine.

JESSE: HIDING OUT IN TENNESSEE

He is having an adventure. It is very seductive and thrilling. He
has changed names many times now. He is hiding out in Tennessee,
a hot night, an old farmhouse, listening to the clock's neurotic met-
ronome, nobody knows where he is. He finds this very moving. He
moves through the Tennessee night and nobody knows where he is.
He changes names.

He investigates things with complete freedom. He looks into
drawers. He is carrying a gun in case somebody interrupts him. He
is the secret agent of a great and important cause, the last of the
underground Confederate Army, the Dixie Mafia, the End of the
World Gang. Everybody down here thinks he is a Mr. Howard, and
the people in Kentucky thought he was a Mr. Woodson, and the
people somewhere else will think he is a Mr. Hite. Behind all these
names is a sentence of death, which he has escaped now three times:
once from fright, once from spite, and once from a desire to show off.

All day long people have been looking at him and choosing what
to think about him, there have been whispers behind his back, he has
nodded amiably at certain statements. But now in the private night
his image and impression is not being appropriated by all the daylight
people who walk the daylight earth down here in Tennessee. Now
nobody knows where he is and so they cannot think about him. Only

he can think about them. He can think about them and watch them from under his hat and choose not to appear to them. He cannot now be robbed of his face or taken to jail or taken aback or think straight. He is not really thinking straight.

It was really just a process of getting rid of his name, and after that his image, and after that his body, and after that his presence. Now what burns in him is match struck at the very center of his brain or mind. A coal-oil lamp is sucking the thick night air into itself in the middle of the table. It's going to be hot all night long. The coal-oil lamp is hot too but he has to have light to disappear by. He realizes he is going through somebody's desk drawers and he has a revolver in his left hand. He's going through Frank's desk drawers. It's a scene. He's having an adventure. You can't have an adventure unless you have a gun. His wife and children sleep as if they were suspended in spring water and the whippoorwill is releasing note after note in a rain of musical fluid. This is what the adventure is all about, it's about Frank. Frank knows his real name. The moon rises from behind a hill, it focuses on Tennessee and out of the mind of the moon walks a blaze-faced sorrel horse. The devil's trumpet flower opens its red mouth and says, *Yes*. Jesse listens as the horse speaks in the language of human beings. Don't talk back. Don't say anything. Because you have abandoned your daylight self with such urgency and such joy, because nobody knows your name, there is the danger of being absorbed by the language of animals.

He realizes he lives among *vegetables*. The oak forest cover, the tulip trees, the standing field corn all night long hacking and sharpening its coarse leaves, down in the bottom fields under the moon. The Cherokee Bukka-man hacks and sharpens his coarse leaves, down in the bottom fields, all night long. Human slavery never seemed to bother him much. It changes names.

Without an identity he begins to grow huge and to evaporate. He can't sit quietly and watch it happen by the light of a coal-oil lamp. It would be a kind of surrender, here in Tennessee, without a name. Without a name anything can take you over, anything can fill you with its language. In his brother's desk he discovers an envelope; it has a name on it, Dick Liddle, and the return address says Richmond, Missouri; evoking the grubby and restless pleasures of Cracker Neck. Gratified, he puts it back. It is a sign. It is a portent. All this night he has been adventuring around without a name, going to and fro in the earth, walking up and down on it. In Missouri something is waiting, but at least he will have a name for it to happen by. "And not even the angels shall know the hour of his coming." Back to Clay County, where at least they will have the right name to put on the headstone. All the visions cloud over and then shatter; he blows out the lamp.

YANKEES IN ST. LOUIS

I

They go into St. Louis on their way back from Tennessee
and stop in a house of ill repute
tending soberly and carefully to their needs.
Sated raptures.
The girls are Irish or at least have no apparent diseases.
It's better than the times around Rocheport and Danville
in 1864. They think, anything is better now than it was
in Rocheport; living in the mud
of the Little Chariton and the spirit will rise
out of the body in spite of everything.
This is what Frank has always counted on.
Frank is always hoping the spirit will rise
out of the body. There were days of nothing
but a kind of sloppy ecstasy, around the river,
sitting on the banks outside Rocheport with the
river rising and rising,

the simple innocence of adolescence;
Boys, let's go burn down Danville.

II

They don't want a pardon.
They stroll through an exclusive neighborhood
dressed soberly in five-button cutaway suits.
There are a lot of rich Yankees around here, says Jesse.
These are not the white-hog Union partisans of Missouri,
these are rich Yankees.
They walk past the Eliot house at 2635 Locust,
on toward the train station at the River.
Jesse says, *What do you bet me, Frank? I bet those people
would spend half a day deciding whether to part their hair
this way or that.* Frank takes his Hamilton watch from
his watch-pocket. *How come they won the fucking war, then,
Jesse?* There is no answer to this at present.

THE IRISH GIRL AT THE PIE DOG HOTEL AND WHORE HOUSE

She has made up stories about the farm and everything, sometimes without even being asked, and decides she doesn't want anything but money anyway. Send out for the evening newspaper, the
Post-Dispatch. Entertaining news of robberies, men running away
with satchels of money. The lace curtains of the Pie Dog Hotel run
inward, printing blue shadows, a new edition every second and the
men from Tennessee are gone. It will be better in a week more or
less when she gets some time off. The light isn't good. That's how
things go. They go fast and in a bad light. Again and again the female
performers lay on a bed and think about their histories. None of them
have good fortune. Or, fortune is for somebody else. Or fortune is for

women without any particular talent and so we specialize in men. Will the electric light tan? Dr. Edmund Beard says no, it won't. *I love to hear the train coming down the tracks with all its symptoms of wanderlust, its horn like a choirmaster sounding the beginning note for a phantom choir that never sings, running up from the bottomlands of the Mississippi, up the Spanish Trace, and the drowned fields of rice and the willow-oak wet and covered with Virginia creeper, the devil's-trumpet vine.* Everything passes by the Pie Dog Hotel in the night, cousins and opportunities, the grass waves in little rivers in the wind of the trains' passage even in the St. Louis yards. She wishes she were grass like that and disembodied. Not to have a body; to leave it behind entirely. If she could sing she would make up a song; "The Irish Girl's Lament." She would be all right if it were not for her body lying on its bed. The body is the copperhead in the haybale, on a wicked frosty morning you split the bale and are struck. She is afraid, looking out the window onto Lafayette Street, that the trains will crash and move across the landscape and not come anywhere near her, that nobody will ever speak to her except as they do. There is just a lot of intolerable noise downstairs (but it is not the news of the world but her own noiselessness) and by now she knows enough to move very quickly into the difficult parts.

TESTIMONY

Dick Liddle, who turned state's evidence at Frank's trial

The baggageman was standing in the side door and Frank seized him by the leg and jerked him out of the car and left him on the ground. The engineer pretended he could not move the train as the brakes were down. We then struck him with a piece of coal and told him we would kill him if he did not start the train. He then threw open the throttle and started it under a full head of steam. Frank jumped up in the cab and stopped it. I went back after Jesse, who was still in the express car. Jesse jumped first and then I followed. We got $700 or $800 that night in packages. It was all good money. Jesse killed McMillan. Frank was in a rage about it. Jesse said, "I thought the boys were pulling out from me. I wanted to make them a common band of murderers to hold them to me."

ASSASSINATION

I

Jesse is not being helped by all his good reasons,
his Black Flags, his secret underground army.
Behind him is a trail littered with corpses.
To other people Kansas City and St. Jo look
    normal
but to Jesse they look like something out of a
penny dreadful, maybe
*Frank Reade, the Inventor, Chases the James Boys
with His Steam Man.*
You never know who has been taken over by these
mechanical devices, the offers of rewards,
Zee or anybody might be one of Them.

The creak of the floorboards and also
turning a page of the *St. Louis Post-Dispatch*
makes a sound so loud
it thunders like distant artillery.
Concentrate on the print, read the
river news:
The river is at 24 feet, 10 inches.
The *Henry Frank* has come in from Memphis
carrying 9,226 bales of cotton, steamboats

are crossing the water, the two sides of
his heart are crashing together with mounting
violence.
By now he only has these two alternatives:
he wonders what it would be like to be killed
        instead,
to be the innocent victim.
He thinks all victims are innocent;
it is familiar and inevitable as a Bible story.
He turns to straighten the picture of a
racehorse, his back
to history, the final solution.

II

Bring on the angels of rain, of newspapers and
celebrating sheriffs, Jesse has reached
his evening.
Now everybody in St. Jo remembers
they sold him coal or shook his hand
or petted his dog.
James W. Graham takes the death picture
with 8 × 11 dry plates;
they had to rope him to a board to get
him upright. There is something strange
about the picture: his fingers appear to
be missing. It was Graham's first day
at work.

III

Jesse's gift was the skill of sundering, parting,
to divide the soul from the body, the flower from
    the
stem, the banks from their money, the being from
the life it held lit and sheltered
in an irreducible heart;
patron saint of the dismembered, the exploded,
the spilled and the broken,

and his last gift was to make a secret of everything.
Zee weeps and sells his guns for groceries:
    —6 dozen eggs at 8 cents a pound
    —1 pound of sugar at 7 cents a pound
    —1 ¼ yards domestic at 15 cents a yard
    —4 ½ pounds of butter.

Everybody splits and
Frank surrenders.

FOUND POEMS

The St. Joseph Western News, May 19, 1882

Robert Ford, the slayer of Jesse James, is the biggest man in Kansas City. He is appearing on the stage three nights a week, for which he is paid $100 a night. The morbid curiosity of the people of Kansas City is beyond human comprehension.

If I could have my body back again
    for a little while, my good old body, the one
that fits the handmade gloves and the riding boots,
everything the way I liked it, what bargain
    can a person make
    nothing to replace it but
    small shines in the shadow of wild underbridges
    a broken china woman in the long pools of the
    Meremec
    the Gasconade,

    think how little I wanted.

I only wanted your money,
the lives of a few individuals nobody
would have heard of otherwise,
    the joy of some derailed trains,
    my name in the *St. Louis Post-Dispatch*,
    the secret life in the backwoods,
    people to shoot,
    cornbread, good horses, Sundays at home,
    the happy splinters of express-car doors
    starbursting into the celebratory air,
the good old boys and the private war cries, our
conspiracy of cruelty and bad manners, the iron
wives we invented at leisure.

What would you give to have my world of limited
    distance
with a safe horizon and no overhead missiles, where
everybody had a biography, a pistol, the old happy
    aggression

we thought would last, like the soil and the rivers,
forever?

You invent murder so big you can't even think
that big.
The planet is so small you can't even think that
small.
I am your last warhead. Behind me is the
evening.

FRANK SURRENDERS: OCTOBER 5, 1882

"I have known no home, I have slept in all sorts of
        places . . . I am tired
of this life of taut nerves . . . I want to see if there
    is not some way out
of this."

Since I was seventeen I have carried
on my person
twenty pounds of iron.

I want to see if there is not
some way out of this.

I am expecting now the approach
of the psalmist, like a sheriff
he will disarm me and speak
his arresting word: Appomattox.

Or I will be a piñata,
and the psalmist, with childlike erratic blows,
will break this heavy clay

and let all my common and inexpensive gifts
rain down on this world, this
private war, this
terrible birthday party.

And now I have made up my mind,
who do I surrender to?
Who will accept these obsolete and heavy
sidearms, who is going to break
my hardshell case with a magic stick?

THE TRIAL OF FRANK JAMES, 1882

As he lays his pistols down on the governor's
    polished desk
we can see him pausing for the photographer
among the globe lamps, facing the man with the
    black hood
on his head, who is using
an 8 × 11 dry plate with a double plate holder.

We, too, are looking for the right authority
to whom we may hand in pistols we do not have
and confess to robberies we have not committed
and apologize to corpses we have not murdered.
We, too, hope for a trial packed with old
    confederates.
We expect, like you, to get off scot-free, revealing
little of our lives or personal disasters before
an admiring crowd

stripped of nothing but our sidearms. You can
    always
buy more sidearms.

If we, too, could find the right one to whom to
    surrender—
but we are choosy—
before whom we could unbuckle everything and lay
    down
our old defenses, drop them
on a mahogany desk, and the Authority, looking on
with mild and kindly eyes, would not know or
    would have
forgotten what we have done,
    unspeakable things
which now seem like nightmares or war footage or
    blue movies.
And the Authority says, That's okay, Frank or
    whatever
your name is, it was a typographical error, you were

assigned the wrong parents, the wrong war, an extra
Y chromosome by mistake.

No one ever says I am your prisoner without
believing somehow in clemency, in mercy
    or in short memories, it is
not something said
by battered wives or people
    held in unnumbered rooms or
children with cigarette burns. It is not said
by those who can no longer talk.

I'll shake hands with anybody that
walks up the road.
At the age of forty-nine almost anybody who
    matters
to me is dead,
in the clean fields
in the simple and uneventful woods,
most by violence.

When I handed in my guns, everything stopped.
It stopped, and there was no more screaming,
the sound of running horses and black powder,
it was all gone.

How slowly people move
and with what patience the horses search
for horseweed in the fields.
I am amazed, I am amazed with what fixed intent
we move from the porch into supper.
I sit down carefully, I am astonished now at
    everything—
the plates with flowers, my big old mother praying
over the food and my shiny hands.
I am free as the unemployed goldenrod and the
    clouds
move in from Kansas, dry and clean.

The Bunceton Eagle, June 25, 1903

Cole Younger, who is associated with Frank James in the man-
agement of a "Wild West" show, is reported to have compelled an
employee to make a refund to a man whom he had shortchanged and
then dismissed the employee. Younger is violating all the traditions of
the circus business and especially the Wild West shows and it will
be interesting to see the result. We guess that Cole considered if
anybody was going to be robbed he would do it himself.

THE LAST POEM IN THE SERIES

The scholar who studies the life of Jesse and Frank
    needs solitude.
This person approaches a cabin through fields and
    some woods, slowly,
seriously, as if they were going there to take vows.
    Everything else
has flown away.

There are no other people.

The flame shapes of cedar and scrub oak are
    drawing something huge and
nourishing out of the clay subsoil, a substance we
    can only guess at.
Johnson grass burns in its low fires, the color of
    prairies. The
sky at this hour and season is a gemmed glass, blue
    and refreshing,
it has raised our broken sight many times before

this. In the cabin
are the voices of the original angers. They wait. It
    is up to the
person who wants solitude to abandon them. If you
    release them they
will fly off like birds or trains. Your skull is very
    small under
the awning of the universe. All the time you walk
    toward the cabin
huge electrons are raining down on you out of the
    heart of the sun.
What do you think of that? Before you can step in
    the door, surrender
and disarm. It is a kind of bank, and can be robbed
    only by the
anti-bandit.

This is the end of the story of Jesse and Frank.
The grass pours by in the white wind like a river
    out of the hill
country, flooding and breaking, and you are
    smoothed by its lengthy
currents.

And so you walk in the door of the bank, your
    hands are empty.

God is only a symbol for life,
for fate or potatoes.
For missing persons smiling out of photographs.
He is more desperate and more commonplace
than once thought. Why is it
we have to fight our way
out of darkness and miscalculation
like a lost patrol in a banana jungle,
    only to discover this,
    the Potato God?

Ah, sweet animism, the silent crystals
at the core of things,
like baseballs and shells, new potatoes,
waiting for moisture,
to spring on you,
    rains of carbon
    and cut glass.

There is another world, close to here,
where people do not stand on the edges.
They live in the middle. Every morning birds with
rust-colored wings untuck and shake off
    the stars that have grown on them. The sun
rises holding screens of pine
in front and the water stirs;
      once: twice.

Everything takes a deep breath.
This is before the bread is baked.
    No one hopes for anything,
these people are ghosts of what went on
before. They have lived through some
blast and were burnt away, they are
without fingerprints, they are like dough.

    They bake themselves brown every morning,
and the sun floats at noon over the single
    street, crisping the tops of their hair.
Only in the night with the rhythmic bark of
a dog does their news reach us,
their smiles, their press releases. That life is
without hope of any kind, that life is
    one day after another, always the same day.
    Expect nothing,
not even the sun.

This man is much taller than I am;
his feet hang out but mine
are still covered
in the middle of the night.

Mostly I look at his shirt pocket;
he can only see
the top of my head.

I can feel his gaze dripping
over my crown like a broken
egg, slithering down.

Everyone is afraid of broken yolks like that,
howler monkeys, guinea hens.

Who knows what men are thinking,
what eggs they are
sticking their long-nailed thumbs into?

You know I have a long, long time seen you coming,
your black, belated stare,
eyes crazy as direction signals, sniper's eyes.
I remember Kansas City, 20th and Vine
where the Blue River Power and Light
left a shine on the rainy clouds,
the hiway out to Denver.
It was a train then;
my nights contained the promise of a train
pulling out
north to the great gray lakes and you were enormous,
big as a boulevard.
Now you have dwindled to the size
of a twelve-year-old
and I have grown too big.
My feet stick out over the ends of beds.

Nothing speaks to us from the whirlwind.
It is the whirlwind itself,
its destructive torrents and vacuumy core
that precipitates these crystals into memory.
I hang onto my consciousness
as if it were a dollar—
the weathermen are regretful. They knew it all along.

Now the hills fold together like playing-cards
aligning their dull colors.
Between them are slices of darkness.
Our fantasies spin and collide
with each other
in the cone of this reality.

I have grown too big for you or anybody,
a natural phenomenon.
And I didn't even mean it,
I didn't mean it at all.

1

We came here by chart and intention,
with calipers and T square, past shoals
marked xx like a kiss with teeth.

Behind us the drowning sound of following waves,
never free of them, waving white fingers
as if saying, good luck. The glib

assumptions of following waves. They dump on
your stern and climb aboard in an uproar of foam
and illegal entry. Our windy destiny like luck
or navigation brings us to this harbor;
False Detour Channel; anxious mariners
wet as laundry.

He is exultant, he finds the place
where we are
on the chart with fingers like calipers
and nautical miles.

At night when we are safe at anchor he opens
a book called *Celestial Navigation*. With this
you can sail the high seas, get straight
to the Solomons. We could turn pirate. You use
a sextant and shoot the sun. It recovers.

2

I'll learn to navigate too, I said.
What if we are sunk in mid-Pacific,
adrift on a life-raft eating turtle.
I should know this nautical magic,

these incantations.
     You wouldn't need to know, he said.
I would take care of that.

     But what if you drown, what if
the killer whales eat you.
Maybe you never
     thought of that.
     Do I make you feel immortal?

She writes in Spanish to someone she knew, but she never knew him very well at all. At her side a list of words that are supposed to mean what she wants to say, along with a picture of the last time she saw him and a Coleman lamp. *I am far away,* she writes, importantly. All over the village the lamps are coming on, people turn up their evening mentality and light themselves, they shine around card games and food.

Actually, I am not so far away; she writes. *I am extremely close.*

This dream is a throwback.
Stars shine through it at the eyeholes.
Why has it come here again?
    The air sticks around its body,
it stands and watches every night,
        its head in the constellations.
Its fingers husk the topknots of the spruce.
    It has patience,
the patience of bones that lay buried
in overhangs,
        skulls with heavy browridges,
waiting in the dead matrix
        for the archaeologist.

For now it is just standing around out there.
    Some day it will begin to speak
only to me,
the insistent whisper
each night
and then it will shout.
Then there will be the fingers
        fumbling at the lock;
it will walk out of the nightmare
with a tearing sound.

"Snow will be used for the inability
of people to communicate
with each other.
It will represent alienation.
We are Canada.
　　We are a cold country."

Are these opinions or commands?
Our words galloped off for the horizon,
　　taking our vocabulary with them.
Since then
　　everyone talks about getting along with others
and improving relationships
　　which can never be solved,
　　only traded in for others.

　　This is the country of the sky,
dilating stars pull brilliance
from outer space,
　　green curtains slide across a mysterious scene,
the borealis
and its moonshow.

　　Once at night I was stopped by a comet,
　　it blew up in green splinters.
　　"This is life in the remote interior,"
　　I said to myself.
　　The shards extinguished separately as they fell.

　　We were awarded this sight
like badges of merit,
campaign ribbons.
　　We grow accustomed to pure hallucination.
The mind is an eye,

it knows something
    it tells only in dreams
    (an arctic ocean
    breaking over frozen bicycles,
fireflies flash in the winter night,
a blacktail deer stands in the white drifts
saying
    this is your mind).

The Washita Mountains crack a long, green eye
As we elbow through in a square and sober semi:
They are only half-awake in their rumpled bedclothes,
Gouges, breaks and bluffs.
This is the hour in the earth's cycle
When metabolisms have run down:
The predator is fed up with chasing, the long-legged runner's
Long legs are folded like jackstraws in a windfall.

The driver is a corncob.
My companion is asleep.
I am a fellow-traveler to ten forward gears
And a Georgia overdrive.
Outside the sweetgrass grows as high as rain
And the morning constellations spin on a stem
Of heat that rises from the plains,

Plains that were flat before
The sea was even salt.
We are gearing down the grades that begin
The long launch to Dallas.
Texas is not my fault.
Sunshine pours from both sides of the horizon at once,
The flyspecked cabwindows are cathedrals of open light.
I am dirty, I am comfortable, I have my boots on.
Sliding down onto the blank and shadeless plains
That burn and burn like chili peppers,
We are deadheading to murderous Dallas.

I approach a school every day, past landscapes and houses I can't recall fifteen minutes afterward. I wear huge dresses of 80 percent polyester and 20 percent cotton, with designs of crushed fried eggs, or maybe they're ruined buildings. My brain is segmented like an ice-cube tray and each segment lasts only so long. I have ten minutes to focus on any one thing and then I go into meltdown. The teacher apparently wants to know what is the major export of Argentina. Doesn't she know? Why is she asking me?

I have no next of kin because I have bought them all tickets to distant places that I found in *The World Book,* and they are not the kind of people who can resist free tickets. Grandad and Lula Belle I have sent to Ulan Bator, under C. Mom and Poppa Daddy opted for Acapulco, under *M,* and my sister was given an excursion ticket to Paris, *F.* Elroy got a bus ticket to Mountain Home, Arkansas, a place seen only in brochures put out by Jimmy Driftwood, where he can shoot squirrels and play pinochle in the secret backrooms of his mind.

I have sent them off special delivery, to flat places in colored half-tone photographs (the women wearing handkerchiefs in wild designs as if they wore their hearts on their heads, their inarticulate, smiling husbands holding market packages or riding down on boars, they are Circassian or Bantu, and behind them the bluish mountains play tones on the observer's soul. Solitude. Excursions), and so they are stamped with goodbye kisses and mailed off into *The World Book.*

I continue to live in the house we abandoned the last time we moved. There are a few things they forgot: three jelly glasses, a high-topped tennis shoe, and there is a drawer lined with newspaper for the knives and forks and spoons, and in it are two parakeet eggs. The newspaper in the drawer says the Slater grain elevator burnt down and Judy Canova is playing at the Sunset Theater. The sun rises out of the Mississippi and sets in western Kansas. Out in the daytime world mysterious normal people walk through shock waves.

Far away are the songs of chickens. The yard is full of petunias and morning glories, butterflies elevate like aftermaths, bits of wallpaper and insulation scattered in the still central air after the explosion. They are graceful and slow, unlike family life, and drift onto morning glories, now folded like gloves.

The World Book has a clumsy, distracted, and episodic devotion to truth, eager under the maroon covers, wanting to be of use; like an eyewitness at civilization's five-car pileup, it offers everything it knows. The perihelion of Mercury is sometimes 36 million miles from the sun. Geronimo died in 1909, and yes! the capital of Argentina is Buenos Aires. In the stillness my mind drifts onto the morning glories, now folded like hands.

But suddenly the family begins to reemerge, it's unfair, everybody has their dream time even in the middle of evacuations, but all of a sudden they are reappearing under the most bizarre headings, *P* for psychology, *M* for myth, the self-absorbed gods and goddesses dressed in bedsheets, sandals, the impossible Demeter grieving, Icarus who burnt and fell, repeating themselves like sales slips.

They have all moved to a town beside the Mississippi, while I have floated sideways in the mind. It is time to go back and inhabit the body's unforgiving house; move on to puberty. Bottles will sparkle and fester in some deep basement. Poppa Daddy will march fearlessly into riverfront taverns, trading used cars with the river bargemen, he will fight and shout and have fun. The only thing left to do before I go back to reality is to make a heading under *Individual* and enter myself there under *I*, write my own section for future reference, and slowly close the doors of the book after me. This encyclopedia includes, after all, *Ethics* as well as *Elizabeth I* and *Eclipse*.

(Look at the black sun's raving white corona!) and here in my mother's house thirty-two years later I discover again Athena in all her improbable armor, Austria's blue mountains, the inner workings of telephones; all the world's false splendor and innocence, which displays its fifth-grade magic as the high-quality stock slides out of my hands.

From this kitchen window we see ravens
seeing us, our breakfast; problems of the
night before.

First the sky, it comes primarily, and under
it flies our desire to be effective, sincere
and saying things easily said.

Better thugs this morning in black
leather feathers, whose joy in garbage
is that of petty criminals breaking
    into the liquor store, ah, scavenging,
it's mankind's highest calling. They say
recycle and so on, but scavenging is
not moral, it's creative.
    Ravens and bears invade the dump,
eating stale cake, playing with
    old lampshades, darkness
and power.
    Eat, eat, there is more.
    We have more.

Raven-like, we perch on the morning.
We sit on our limbs and make sounds like
bending metal.
We recount the first year we began to shrink
(we remember), grow oil-slick, speak
    like birds, rise
on available currents and swim
    in available light.

You will be jacked into the air
until your beveled face appears
in my steaming mirrors.
Sit down under my white towel,
the pressing, experienced finger
that deals in foams and small change.

I have a drawer full of old watches,
wire-rim glasses that no one fits,
a settled bitter medicine gone brown.
My scissors lay about like a
bushwhacker—how do you like yourself?

You sit, clam-faced and sticky. I whip off
the white towels, the striped sheet, with
the expectant bravado of a mayor
revealing a stodgy monument for the first time
to a cheering crowd.
I am standing on your hair.

I release the lever. You descend from an
        enormous height.
A little short, I'm sure, but
it always grows back. It's so thick
and brown—lion-colored. Don't be sad.

You will experience yourself in a familiar way,
your hair like nerves clipped and fit.
Already the blunt stumps lie down
and align themselves.

Who are these people I married
    and abandoned?
I must have had five husbands by now,
    like that woman at the well,
and the man I am with now,
he is not one.

I live on a gravel farm in apple country,
    where people don't talk about
the knives in their backs,
the bloodstained coveralls.

Cards arrive from the Spanish Sahara.
    "Remember me?"
Do I ever.
    These selves abandoned,
these old photographs.
    When I married I was someone else,
but all the divorces
were me.

I am handing you a cup of coffee.
It has my hands around it,
a white, nervous clutch of steam.
Your face is set, like a table,
to receive it.
The color of your hands is poor-white
their silence smoothes over inappropriate remarks.
The conversation becomes
a series
of X-rays
on knuckles
and a cabbage-green kitchen
and the forehead that dwindles
to a point.
Am I a thin man or
the obedient, peeling wallpaper
stained shut?

The air freezes; it cracks panes
into designs like chicken-wire and I see the
    street through it
which winds and dries its salt. In the
    garment district, a man
with the sad skins of mink and lynx
    over his shoulder
rustles to an appointment.
The North blooms here like a rattling
    silicone-flower, white-refractive
and prismatic, icing over the corneas
    of those who dare to look.
Rhinestones accrete the eaves.
The night becomes creamy and powder-blue
    with apostrophes of silence.

A door opened to another world
and a blue heron flew out.

A canoe sailed into the epicenter
and turned to glass.

The film that runs always in the brain stalls and burns
its image. Trees fell into ovens, a design in black

was fired onto the face of the earth, and over this water,
this solution of ash and acid, we travel between

the pages of a new world, filling in blanks, voices (where
there were none) noises (where the wind pulls a long note

of silence through black flutes).

My head is stuck in a large, five-pointed star.
It is wired for neon.
Beyond it lie endless possibilities
but now its simple-minded shape
reminds me of the 34,080 hours I spent
in damp classrooms, made of children,
wood, and negative writing.
I betrayed my friends by becoming catatonic;
my chintz clothes tied themselves on me every morning.
My friend the epileptic foamed and snapped
but the teacher read on anyway,
her voice like a pill
soothing my nerves.
Sometimes I wondered whose nerves they were.

My sister is a child again
and has a baby.
I must take her somewhere safe.
    We are located in the depths of my mind,
perhaps the medulla.
    Will we never get out of here, this
gray atmosphere of brain and smoke?
Somewhere up above there is light.
    We are all wounded.
    Several detectives want my information
but we continue like war refugees
    toward my right hemisphere.
We will keep on these rotten steps upward
    until we reach the airport tower
and at last look out of the long plate windows
    at the thunderous jets landing,
taking off,
landing,
taking off.

The clock's hands dislodge hours—
sticking them to the walls.

I never notice them until
strangers bang at the door,
newspapers replace themselves,
and my associates begin to fold their
    lives into tidy squares.

Now they are in my eyes, shifting
in batik patterns.
I see my life

through a clear pane of minutes and hours
like the faceted spectacles of flies,
those nitwits, their quick
garbagey lives.

But it is the rope itself
full of lunatic assertions
that electrifies the hanger-on with the insistence
of a heart attack;
there is always the hope this world
might be less normal than it appeared;
these slow considerations have
changed my heavy head.
Hand over hand, I am
getting you on the end of the line.
Hello, you fast talker.
Guess who this is.

Fat, bristling heads wind toward the sun like radar.
Heads heavy as dynamite,
drooping like stones on green straws,
they grapple with colored soils
from Galveston to Yellowknife
on the long clearing-ground up the center
      of the continent.

It is a long walk, passing the still, nappy
      ranks of sunflowers.
They nod, a carpet of eyes.
They are not bored.

A house, stiff as crepe-paper and wrinkled,
lives at the edge of the sunflowers.
Every night a woman sleeps there
surrounded by them,
her mind on Arcturus, her children peeping from
      under the doorstone.
Every day brings her closer to some disaster.
It waits, like a sunflower
blind and stiff.

OPENING SCENE

She is entraining for the east somewhere, as Myrna Loy and Jean Arthur and Carole Lombard used to entrain on the Twentieth Century Limited, walking down the concrete apron beside the large cars— minor characters exiting stage left and arriving stage right—with matching luggage and a hat with feathers and a porter reaching for her bags. You've seen it a million times in black and white: steam whistling out from between the teeth of the wheels, very swank and prebomb. She's finding it easier to depart and effect closure, to become impermeable, like a trench coat, to *not care* about leaving somebody, to *not care* even if it was her fault (and of course it was her fault); finding it easier to cease something than to start another new thing, to leave America than to escape to Canada.

THROUGH THE GATE

A distinguishing characteristic of "hard-boiled" detective fiction is that the heroines, who are always tramps of some utterly enchanting sort, are rescued and forgiven by the hard-boiled one and made pure again, usually by violence and repentance. Violence and repentance: major cultural characteristics of Americans with their Movietone memories, including hers, as she walks through Gate Four struggling with her bags, too confused to find a redcap, and the porters saying, "Car 129? Straight ahead, ma'am."

FOREIGNERS ETC.

And now she is almost running, afraid of her misdemeanors back there across the border in America; but she has faith in herself. She has the capacity to invent stories, as long as she has an audience, as long as she has you, the reader, for whom to invent them. They are often outrageous lies, having gone beyond the bounds of "story," but they are engaging and oddly believable.

I'll make my way to Montreal and meet him or somebody there. Every-thing will work itself out. What life on a Canadian train needs is some vigorous presence, some dash; a few lies, inventions, a script, a shooter, a storyboard, depth of field; whatever it is, it's starring Katharine Hepburn.

She is almost running, trying to remember that she is in another country; she's in a *province.*

MINOR CHARACTERS; THE MINK COAT

British Columbia, a province, begins on the west coast with a dinner of rain; then it has a few drinks. If the sea could rise, it would. She is too tall to be of any comfort to short men and she's wearing a navy pinstripe suit and a pillbox hat with a face veil. Secondhand treasures. She imagines herself in her favorite 1940s movie; love those train scenes.

I've got a secret bank account, astronomical debts, a chariot of fire, and a gift certificate to the treasure of the Sierra Madre. I'm an African Queen and I've got a spare heart that works.

This is the kind of thing you've got to tell yourself after having been fired, after a divorce, after walking out on him, after running up an immense amount of credit card debts, after having left Seattle on an impulse, after having gone to Vancouver and bought a series of train tickets on your Visa which will take you across unknown prov-inces; this is the kind of thing you have to tell yourself. Then you won't get depressed, or desperate; you won't have around you that shiny aura of somebody who doesn't know where their next train ticket is coming from. She is determined to stay cheerful, and anyway she's leaving everybody for a remote city called Montreal. It's raining in west coast buckets, and as she is helped up the steps the mahogany mink coat goes damp and sulky; it seems to know it hasn't yet been paid for. Mink are creatures of water and earth and don't believe in plastic cash. *Never mind,* she runs behind the porter to her compart-ment. *Just never, never mind.*

The Vancouver train station is a construction of 1890 dignities and recent decorative blunders. In the park outside there are great architectonic oak trees, and in one corner a catalpa tree hanging all over with green bean pods like syllables, eternally waving its fat round leaves at eternally arriving and departing trains. Now, with the wind, it turns its back on the whole idea and drops catalpa-bean capsules, as if it were a junkie suddenly discovered by police: *open up in there!* The catalpa tree throws up its hands, and the train whistles, and begins to move, and pigeons take off like applause.

The transcontinental moves out of the moist city of Vancouver, leaving behind the city's rainy sea-buses and its steam clock, people in Kerrisdale buying red Princess phones, others in North Vancouver wondering where they left their ironing-board covers, people in the East End always trying to get across Hastings alive; some do. She is not thinking about her debts, or the computers busily filing her several names, about skip-tracers in Canada in pursuit of American cash. She is not thinking about how and when she will go to sleep (it will be somewhere on a train, moving) or how maybe this time the insomnia will evaporate, or how in her dreams the remnants of the imaginations of suicides—like gasoline rags, potentially combustible—will slide down out of the ether just above her dreams. Coming halfway down the stairs of the mind and then going back up again. And then coming back down again. No flames.

REASONS OF HER OWN

For reasons of her own she wants to evoke that era of the forties when daring heroines in mink jackets and pillbox hats got on trains, that safe past before mass extinctions and hidden toxins. When Amelia Earhart got into an airplane and disappeared forever, when Lauren Bacall went to the Caribbean to buy a hat and departed. That was

To Have and Have Not. Like most people she confuses real events in the past with events on film; call her, Our Heroine.

AMERICAN MONEY

American money is narrow and long like Virginia Woolf's feet. American money is disappearing into electronic devices where it can't say anything anymore with its pyramid eye. American money disappears down the ratholes of artillery; stuck in the electronic lockup, American dollars are becoming evasive and shy.

She feels she has liberated fifty thousand of the little prisoners, put them back into circulation; they are all working for her and productive. Where to go next? Maybe she'll go and liberate some Honduran dollars, help them with their international debts; or maybe Mexico. She's heard that if you put ten thousand American dollars in a Mexican bank you could simply live off the grateful interest the Mexican government would present to you. It's a thought, anyway.

CANADIAN MONEY

Canadian dollars are blue, green, red, orange, violet and brown. Sometimes all on the same bill. They fold up in her billfold like the colors of exotic confusion. Technicolor money. They display Mounties on horses, carrying lances, pointed inward in a circle of black animals. They brag about their purple oil refineries, they revere mountain lakes. Blue fishing boats sail off into an azure maritime sea. You are invited to spend them on American products, American movies, American televisions and American books. She will do none of these things. She will take a Canadian train. Happy landings to you, Amelia Earhart.

UNEMPLOYMENT IN HEAVEN

Also getting on the train are a group of Americans, apparently having fallen out of the United States the way minor angels fall out of clouds every time there is unemployment in heaven.

Well, what do they know?

People make observations on her life all the time, as if they were up in the Dome and her life were sliding by outside them and they were being asked to comment on it. And they could say, "That's a nice mountain," or "I don't find this part of the Great Plains very interesting." She has plans of running away from everything and becoming a charming drunk. But how to go about it? It's expensive!

Charge it.

CHANGES

The Americans are from Baton Rouge and Houston. They are going to play Clue all the way across Canada. The train is going to simply keep going, the landscape is going to fall into place, the tracks are going to align themselves with absolute precision from here to Halifax, and the brightest proposition of all is the mysterious city at the end of her journey. It's mysterious because she doesn't know which city it's going to be. Call her, Our Heroine. And as the porter carries her matching pigskin luggage into Compartment C she glances at the Americans down in the lounge, and decides not to tell them she is an American too, only changed. She wants to be the only American aboard. She came up here to get away from Americans. She liked the thought of "British Columbia," *La Colombie Britannique.* How could anybody resist a *province,* and especially a province with a second French name like that? Both French and western; it's kind of swank, really. The porter did not tell her he, too, was changed; only French.

FALLING IN LOVE WITH HATS

The VIA Rail transcontinental has a blunt blue-and-yellow head on it which will drive through sheer mountain walls and extend its long neck into the stretches of the east, carrying her with it, effortlessly. Nobody will know where she is. The porter drops her bags on the floor of Compartment C on the *Algonquin Park,* the very end car of the train. She hands the porter a Canadian two-dollar bill; he holds it up by the tail and sneers at it and seems to be about to throw it off the train. Or maybe just drop it on the floor and step on its head and put it out of its misery. Finally he tucks it in his red jacket pocket and exits like a stage direction. Alone (at last). The pause of waiting and halted, frozen departure. Not quite going yet, but with one wheel almost going and the train paused, poised, just about to. Just about to. She looks at herself in the triple mirror over the dressing table. "I love this hat," she says to her trinity of personalities. "I just love this goddamn hat."

ENTER THE HERO; LONG SHOT

The dressing table has three mirrors, all of them accurate as gun sights. The train shrieks around the curves of the Fraser Canyon and she puts her shoes up where it says *Chaussures* and her bags up where it says, she thinks, *Les Bags*; and all that French is just another reassurance that she's in *another country,* a border between her and all those debts, and so it's safe now to go out to the lounge for a drink. The passengers back there are gasping as they look over the immense and serious drops of the Fraser Canyon, down into the recesses of China Bar—the sunlight sinking and gurgling as if it were leaking away down some celestial drainpipe—and she suddenly feels that the train is stopping. It must stop itself car by car in a long series of blue vertebral halts. A small sign stands up beside the track; it says CHINA BAR. She sees a man in a fedora and a big long dirty coat swing aboard the train two cars ahead, carrying a grip.

Why has the train stopped for this man?

For the plot, of course.

For the plot and for the polarity, for his battered case and his face and his way of occupying space; that's why the train stopped. Hiatus. Pause. Pause steam, pause wheels, pause *whistle!* And starts and repeated starts all down the cars. They are moving forward again, in a long series of blue vertebral charges into Hell's Gate. And suddenly she is assured that this Canadian train, with its end panels showing Acadian farmers with baskets of apples, cheeky blond equestriennes riding behind a guide through the Rocky Mountains, all done in tones of gray and pink and Rose of Sharon sometime in the middle fifties, is invested with a *romantic presence*. Like the man in the Camel advertisements; like photographs of photographers taking photographs surrounded by admiring Pathans; like lies, prevarications, inventions, illusions, stories, pacifiers, anything you can think of that causes human beings to act like idiots; a *romantic presence*.

REMEMBER THAT; SEE YOUR DIAGRAM

See your diagram for the mystery to unfold satisfactorily.

On page three is a diagram of the last car on the transcontinental, one of the old Park cars with their aging 1950s splendors. There is a sunken bar behind frosted glass, the glass depicting Canadian ducks being startled out of their wits by some unseen and ominous presence; and in the lounge area are armchairs made of pink carpeting and tube steel, newspapers and battered ashtrays. The end of the car is round, with a porch, the place from which movie stars and royalty used to wave or declaim things to each other. There are also, in the end car, four bedroom compartments: A, B, C, and D. Hers is Compartment C. Remember that.

And when she saw him get on the train at China Bar, she quickly slammed shut her window blind and turned around, and surprised herself in the full-length mirror on the back of the door. She picked up her pillbox hat and put it on her head as if it would save her from poverty and tallness and old age, from death and lonesomeness, from all the terrors of Hell's Gate, which they are rapidly approaching.

(Well, *something* does. *Something's* got to save you. Why not a hat?)

Get the diagram and check it out, because it is here the drama will be played out. As in a game of Clue the reader is supplied with a diagram which can be seen as the various compartments of the reader's mind, where huge symbols and stereotypes crash into each other, run in and out of the doors of the left and right brain, blundering like butlers and detectives, vamps and rich widows, a Western Union girl in saddle shoes and Mr. Boddy, without whom none of us would be here.

"Ladies and gentlemen, in a little while we'll be passing through

Hell's Gate," says the conductor, ripping off half their computer tickets with wild abandon, and everybody loooooookkkkkksss out.

A SHIT JOB

He is reading a report when he hears the train approaching in the distance. It has to slow down at China Bar, that offbeat bottleneck in the Fraser Canyon, a heart in a slow artery. All around him his story exists like boxcars, with no effort. He has not constructed his own story. The paper is crackling and trying to escape in the rising wind of the canyon. The report says:

This woman appears to be traveling across Canada by train, posing as a railroad detective, claiming to solve mysteries that not only have the other passengers not seen as mysteries at all, but in which they are completely uninterested, such as:

Who are we, really?
Why are we here?
Where are we going?
What is the purpose of your life? and
Why am I asking you this?

She is usually dressed in vintage hats, suits, as well as expensive and tasteless haute couture; evidence of fraud. She is not always dangerous if apprehended, not always alert if questioned, not always defensive if accused, and is not always broke or fired, but usually. May be continuing to use Visa, MasterCard, and American Express; will most likely disembark somewhere east of February carrying everything she owns in spite of herself.

What a shit job, he thinks. I can't really be doing this.

INSTANT REPLAY OR: CAN YOU RUN THAT BY AGAIN?

And when she saw him swing onto the train at China Bar, she quickly slammed shut her window blind and turned around, and saw

herself in the full-length mirror on the back of the door—NOW AP-
PEARING—like a special attraction and a surprise. She picked up her
pillbox hat and put it firmly on her head as if it would save her from
tallness, from being old or dead or poor or lonesome, from all the
suicidal terrors of Hell's Gate, which they are now approaching.
(Well, *something's* got to save you. Why not a hat?) And he seems to
have seen her, his face shadowed by his hat brim, a five o'clock
shadow, a six o'clock shape.

"Ladies and gentlemen, we are now passing through Hell's Gate,"
and everybody looooooooookkksss out.

She steps out into the aisle and walks down to the bar behind the
frosted glass, and says to the bartender:

"I'll have a rum and Karma-Kola."

The bars of sunlight are falling one after the other into the Fraser,
falling like the slats of a venetian blind, and the Americans are already
setting up the complex murder-mystery game called Clue. Someone
will be found out, someone will be discovered in the hot ambushes
of the *deed,* and one person or another will lose. There is some
music playing, a series of notes like spring run-off, now freezing into
fall, and the mountain poplars are spending their yellow coins like
gamblers.

DELAYED IMAGES

The man who got on at China Bar walks into the club car; he
walks down the aisle, puts his grip into Compartment D (remember
that) and looks down to the bar beyond the frosted glass. And there
she is:

Sitting in the Club Car Drinking Rum
and Karma-Kola,
like a book title.
Is this a detective novel or what?

His effortless story falls into place, a series of delayed images.

She continues to make hers up, spending her imaginative energy
like a gambler.

He sat down across from her and took off his hat, which was very old, and brushed off the front of his jacket, which was careworn, and looked at his watch, which was a big one with hands on it; and it was six-thirty in the evening. They were passing by the stone ramparts and foaming liquid theologies of Hell's Gate. She glanced out the window and thought about the mechanics of ending it all (all what?— it was something Lupe Velez never asked herself, caught between the sudden apostrophes of sunset and terror) and said to the man,

"But where are you really from?"

and he said,

"Why not from China Bar?"

and she said,

"Because it doesn't look like anybody really lives at China Bar, and because of your watch."

It was a shot in the dark, and she knew she was not likely to hit anything, not with the amount of dark she was shooting into.

"What about it?"

"It says seven-thirty. That means you've just dropped in from another time zone, say Alberta."

"Alberta," he said, agreeably. And then, "Right." And he asked her,

"Who are you?"

and she said,

"I'm a railroad dick."

PARENTHESES

(What, no opening gambits? Like:

"Where are you going?"

"Montreal. Where are *you* going?"

"Same place. It's a long trip."

"Three days and three nights. But it's nice having a compartment."

"Yes, it is. I especially like having a compartment on this end car."

"Yes. There are only four of them." (see diagram)

Pause. Pause drink, pause squeal of wheels; hiatus.

"Mine's C."

"How odd. I'm in D."

They realize they are in for three days and three nights on the old *Algonquin Park,* over the mountains and the Connaught Tunnel, the Kicking Horse Pass, in for Calgary, Regina, Winnipeg, Thunder Bay, Toronto; in it for the duration, for what it's worth.

She will make up her own story in direct contradiction to what was made up for her. He makes up his own story as an enhancement of the one that was made up for him. So there you are. This is how they strike each other; like a match and a sandpaper surface. End of parentheses.)

A CLASSY EXIT

"Oh really?" He looks over at her hat and her tacky secondhand clothes and the mahogany mink: a jarring mix of signals. He takes her drink from the stand and sniffs it. "A railroad dick drinking some kind of cosmic Kool-Aid." They look out over the landscape, where the ground has risen up out of the Fraser Canyon toward more agreeable mountains. She takes stock; she is sitting in the club car beside a large, fortyish man with a day's growth of beard and sweaty clothes who seems to be looking for something. Maybe he's lost his twin sister or his options; maybe he has a story that he's made up all by himself, but she doubts it. She wonders if he's going to turn out to be Dull Normal, and if he does, how she can get away. But he wants to know, "Have you ever arrested anybody?"

"Of course." She rises to the challenge of inventing another lie for yet another stranger. "I just arrested a guy last week for homicide in a no-homicide zone."

He snorts; it appears to be a form of laughter. "But aren't you supposed to find things out?"

She's got to think up something else here. Okay, she's got one; it's easy. "I just found out last week that Clark Gable had false teeth."

"Not bad," he says. "That's really not bad."

Oh, bizarro, she thinks. *This is turning into plain icky regular prose fiction.*

What can you do but get up and walk away from it when things are turning plain icky and regular?

"Excuse me," she says, and gets up and walks out of the bar in time to some very offbeat rhythms: a classy exit.

LEFT ALONE

He asks the bartender for a drink from the first bottle his eyes light upon behind the bar. The train is going through evening like a detective through somebody's drawers. There's a final indecency in the pursuit of American capital as it slides across the permeable border, even when it's as arresting as this one. Pursuits have to be worth it; there's got to be something at the end which will make you bigger or more complicated than you were, something which is unambiguously rewarding. In his crude pursuits and captures there has always been the chance of watching the performances of fright or regret, naked people thinking naked thoughts. At this point he doesn't believe he could detect elephant shit in a henhouse. He leaves everything leavable on the table (peanuts, change, a clue), a fort deserted in panic or boredom; he walks away from the Americans playing at butlers and fiends toward Compartment D. Remember that.

KICKING HORSE

We've all had our moments of terror. They are usually when (a) we think we may be killed and (b) we think we may be taken for who we really are.

That night they move through Salmon Arm and Revelstoke; they are through Roger's Pass and are now climbing the grade toward Kicking Horse, the highest pass at the spine of the Rockies. They have gone into the spiral tunnel moving upward, the laborious train moving and moving upward, and she dreams of The Man from China Bar. She dreams he has a list of questions for her; she dreams he has a watch that always says an hour ahead of the real time, that inside his watch night is moving forward faster and faster, accelerating, infinitely accelerating, as if they were on the edge of a black hole, as if they were detectives researching the possibility of infinite night! She dreams his face is hidden under the brim of his hat; she dreams her own face is hidden behind her veil; she dreams the train is moving upward and always upward through the spiral tunnel toward Kicking Horse Pass, and then suddenly and horribly dreams that her ears are bleeding, that her pillow is covered in blood; and she says something very loud and sits upright, throwing the pink woolen Canadian Pacific blankets on the floor; and the train is turning on itself inside the spiral tunnel, introverted, clanking and jerking. The porter knocks on the door and says,

"Ma'am, are you all right?"

The Man from China Bar can't help but hear all this through the thin paneling; he hears her say,

"Oh yes? What's wrong?"

and the porter says,

"You must have had a nightmare, ma'am,"

and she says,

"Well, what was it about, do you think?"

and he says,

"Ma'am, I have no idea,"

and she says,

"But wait, where are we now?"

and the porter says,

"In a spiral tunnel in the heart of a mountain, moving upward toward the day, toward a very high pass in the peaks, and we'll be there soon, and we'll stop briefly to take on a cargo of light, so be of good heart, my darling, and do not be afraid, because we will not be going around in circles in the dark forever," and she says, "Oh I'm so glad." Rocked on the slow climbing of the coaches and all their hubcap-shaped wheels, eight to a car.

OVER THE KICKING HORSE

Porters in their red jackets move smoothly and efficiently throughout the train—the Ministers of Sleep and Dreams, with their small packages of soap and matches, and their penlights, towels and toilet paper—silently handing out in the night all your images and nightmares. Men of great circumspection, stepping without noise on their crepe soles, carefully, with a sense of *movement*: of a train and of *moving persons*. When the train emerges from the spiral tunnel and at last reaches the top of Kicking Horse Pass, they walk to the aisle windows and look downward in the glittering high-altitude moonlight to the three different levels of track below.

And then they go on, moving down the racketing and rolling train while outside the windows on either side there is an infinitude of spaces and peaks, with an edgy shine to it all, generative, like a mind in near space, cloud banks foaming in the moonlight below as if here— at the top of the Canadian Rockies—were where all the weather of North America were generated: this is where clouds are manufactured; this is where lightning is forged; this is where rain is distilled in long, flashing tubes of moon; the mint where snowstorms are printed and impressed, where sundogs are cobbled and walked off with like the shoes of the sun in reaching twenty-four-hour steps. The porters move silently with flashlights from car to car, dispensing dreams and nightmares, picking up the tossed blankets of the sleeping car passengers and regretting the tortuous positions in coach, whispering, "Be of good heart, my darlings, there are miles of it, and it is still the same earth."

'TI DEJEUNER

The first call for breakfast serves as a wake-up call for those who have come from British Columbia; the shocking voice of the dining car attendant as he storms through the sleeping cars, "FIRST CALL FOR BREAKFAST, PREMIER APPEL POUR LE 'TI DEJEUNER!!" urgent and controlled, as if you must wake up now! Or forever miss the town of Canmore with its bare November trees full of wrens, the arena, a gabled house with a red Toyota in front, a cowboy on a bicycle.

(They passed a freight in the early dawn light, and the rhythm of sunflashes between the cars was a pulse; it awakened him briefly, leaving him with the impression of discontinuity and the sensuous arrival of day. What's his story? Where's he really from? For that matter, where are *you* really from? What are these long argyle socks doing in the sink, drooping over the edge, plaid pythons; and what are the rattling crashes of the window frames doing waking him so early, the drumming passage of a freight, or was it the dining car attendant with the piercing voice whom he would like, right now, to strangle? He turns over in bed, he hears her turning over in bed; he imagines they are facing each other through the thin paneling as if they were in two different frames of a love comic.)

ADDRESSES: THE MAN FROM CHINA BAR

His address is, at this point, nothing but train. On a stretch of bad track his entire past falls out of the overhead rack and spills on the floor like underwear or playing cards.

"Drop something in there, sir?" says the porter, who was passing by out in the aisle.

"Yes, but it's all right," says The Man from China Bar. Lying on the carpet is his identification, the real one, and his purposes, which are large and high-caliber. He shoves it all back into his suitcase. He looks at his shoelaces, which cross each other like two single-minded arguments, and wonders how he got here, wearing feet like this.

OUR HEROINE AT A DISADVANTAGE

On the morning of the first day after the first night on the train, she comes up out of vital nightmares about large, empty containers. She has such a hard time with herself: the self that was delighted as a Christmas child with the cornucopia of plastic cash; the self that was hidden behind a hat (O Karma! O Maya! O Illusion! O This! O That! O the Other!); and the self that can be toted up on a running balance at the bank, the credit companies, all those organizations that have your number; and the self that goes riding on trains, the one that sat in the club car the night before drinking rum and Karma-Kola; and another, startling self that opens your compartment door and then closes the door behind it, saying,

"Good morning," and hands her a styrofoam cup of coffee. And the self that says,

"What are you doing in my compartment?"

And the self that says,

"You should keep your door locked. I came to see if you were going to breakfast. And I see you aren't yet, or you'd be dressed."

If somebody does something unacceptable and yet hands you a gift, like a cup of coffee, at the same time, you are very likely to take the gift and your anger will defuse, go out, be rained on by the generosity of his hand with the coffee in it. He settles himself comfortably on the floor in the corner, apologetic and sincere, in a rattling patch of sunshine. She tries to drink the coffee without letting the sheet slide down, and the train is following its natural bent toward Calgary. What the hell is she supposed to do? Talk? Be intelligent?

"Well, I am going to breakfast but why don't you leave first, and then I can get dressed."

"Drink your coffee," he says, "and give me the cup."

She's at a disadvantage; she can't remember people very often seeking her out and giving her something, although she has worked very hard at giving the opposite impression. They have both worked very hard at making themselves into the right stereotype. Neither one of them has always been completely successful.

LYING ON TRAINS

The engineer has decided to gain the time they lost coming over Kicking Horse and is pressing the red zone. They are rocketing along the Bow River at an awesome rate of speed, and The Man from China Bar opens the hard-to-open 1953 door for her into the snow-powdered vestibule, where everything is candied with frost and glaze, and the next car is a Pullman; they pass the bunks and bunks of sleepy people, and the beautiful old fading colors of Canadian trains, and the sleeper's *ultra-monde* hues and tints of dreams that are just now sliding away into breakfast.

"But what do you do for a living?" she asks The Man from China Bar. They stand at the entrance to the dining car, hesitant as fish entering new rapids.

"Sound," he says. "I was a sound tekkie on an Australian movie last winter."

"I don't believe it," she says. "People always lie so terribly on trains."

And she heard him laughing.

INSTANT REPLAY

She doesn't have on all that vintage 1940s today. All she wanted was that scene, that one scene that had been growing in her mind for months; she calls it *boarding the train.* Now she's wearing expensive labels and other clothes she bought on charge accounts after she got fired, after she left him, after she decided. There's nothing wrong with Royal Robbins that a little money wouldn't cure. Her hair falls down her back like a lot of wilderness resisting agriculture.

"Sound," he says as the waiter ushers them to a table. "I was head sound tekkie on an Australian film a year ago this fall."

"I don't believe it," she says. "People always lie so subtly on trains."

And she could hear him laughing.

BREAKFAST IN CANADA

As they are having their breakfast they watch the other sleepy people around them: people from the sleeping cars smoothing their hair, the ones from coach looking as if they had spent the night in a duck press. She and he gaze out of the armor of their stereotypes as the Bow River slides past in as many loops as a snake might exhibit locked in its winter tangle, in all the colors between green and indigo, cascading toward the low, glossy, yellow-and-white prairie land-scape—*so Canadian,* so utterly cherishable, like pear cider, like a photograph of your mother when she was twenty-one—and she is telling him all about herself.

"When I was little, in Missouri, my cousin Rita Jean and me used to be put to bed together out on my Aunt Hetty's back porch, and we would talk about getting out of Missouri, and where we would go, and what we would do if we got out. The trouble was, we didn't know what we would *do.*"

"A lot of people have that trouble and don't even know it."

"Yes, exactly, that's what I told Rita Jean. And we didn't know what kind of men we were supposed to try to get and marry us, outside of the kind of men we were raised with, and if they didn't beat you up and they let you drive the car, what else could you want?"

"Nothing, obviously."

"And we used to lay there in my Aunt Hetty's feather bed out on the back porch, sleeping out there even in the middle of winter, and the feather bed was so deep we'd have to holler at each other across the puffs of it; it was like talking to each other on the telephone. And we could see all the winter stars, and we could see the pear tree by the pond with the little pear twigs all sticking around like fish bones and the stars blossoming in them instead of pear flowers, and we'd say, 'If I ever get out of Cooper County I ain't never coming back.'"

"Well, did you?"

"Oh, I go back all the time!"

It occurs to her they are speeding through counties right now, all of which people want to leave, or some do; or do they have counties in Canada?

"Do you all have counties in Canada?"

"Sometimes."

He listens so carefully that she thinks he may be comparing her to a description in some report that says she skipped out on $50,000 worth of bad paper. Suddenly she feels she should explain everything about her life, so he would understand why she skipped out on $50,000 worth of bad paper, but she doesn't. *Stop imagining things,* she tells herself. *On the other hand, if I stopped imagining things, I never would have done this; life would be dreadful. But anyway, he's just an attractive man that happened to get on the same train I did, is all.*

"What else do you do besides sound?" she asks.

"That's all. Sound. I listen my way through life."

A HEART IN RESERVE

The dining car moves with the heated steams of cooks and heavy railroad silver—old Canadian Pacific silver—and you can get breakfast splits of champagne but you have to push it because behind all the frosted glass etched with kingfishers and meadowlarks and the man in Canadian Pacific's Tuscan-red jacket, there's that apparent and careful sobriety of a northern country. Only the Trans-Siberian runs a longer distance, and at what cost! But after sobriety comes a deeper sobriety, that of a final, happy gaiety that comes when you know you've stepped off some edge, a tectonic plate; you're running headlong across a continent and being served breakfast at the same time. She's an African Queen, and if she's careful, she keeps a heart in reserve.

"I thought you would be interesting when I saw you," he said, "and you are."

How can she resist this?

What does he mean, *interesting?*

INVENTING YOUR OWN STORY

The Man from China Bar says he has spent the summer, after doing the sound for the Australian movie, trying to shoot the Fraser in a Volvo. That's why he was at China Bar. For the first time, he finds himself having to invent his own story. Make it up, single-handed—without the cooperation of secretaries, mothers, wives, girl-friends, advertising—and suddenly he wants to tell her, *I didn't used to be this way. I had a different job at one time and then something happened. I didn't always have this occupation.*

He glances at her; maybe it's not her. Maybe the woman he's looking for is really evil, a chippy as it were, a professional who knows how to juggle credit cards and forge signatures, a nasty Seattle booster, a paperhanger, somebody with a dull creepy mind who labels everyone she knows as either a *scumbag* or *a real sweetheart*; someone he could simply arrest in mid-flight and return to the authorities and the credit companies. *I didn't always have this occupation,* he wants to tell her. He wants to invent a story as to why he took it up. A tragedy in his past somewhere. Like Dashiell Hammett had tragedies. Or invented them. He watches her suddenly grow nervous and light another cigarette, look at him and then look away.

"Where are we now?" she asks, looking out.

"We just passed through a town called Harris." He pushes the plate of sliced fruit toward her. "Eat your breakfast. This may be the last mango in Harris."

She bursts out laughing, spewing smoke, and he thinks: *it can't be her.*

RAILROAD SILVER

She wants to get out of breakfast. The Man from China Bar sits there with his past around him—uncertain and suspended, as hers is—like those of everybody on the train. If one were to note down what was really said it would read like a musical score, rushing toward Calgary. But he says very little. This is because he's a sound man, probably. And in his silences she will talk too much. Or say something factual even when she doesn't mean it. She gets up from the steam and the carnations, the heavy cups and the thin waiters and the railroad silver, the glossy flat landscape and the coiling loops of the Bow River—which has apparently fallen out of heaven just as it is, a celestial lariat—and says,

"Really, I must get back to my compartment and write some letters."

And he says,

"Something's wrong. I can hear it in your voice." And in his head he says, *Wherever you're from, don't be from Seattle.*

And she says,

"Yes, well, sometime you must describe it to me. I can't really hear the sound of my own voice."

ON HOLD

She feels they've been sitting in the Calgary train station too long. She's getting nervous; she is wondering if somebody has spotted her and they're waiting for confirmation of her description from the credit companies or something? Are we moving yet? Is anything going to happen yet? Downtown Calgary appears to have been built over Labor Day weekend out of shiny stuff. The train is still halted; has been for hours. They are suspended; prepared to go but not moving. It is as if it were midnight of the New Year when something is supposed to change forever, if only the whole train of the year's months would move forward. By the time they get to where they're going all the passengers will be jaded with movement and noises but now everybody is thinking *Let's go.* There is one last passenger running down the concrete apron, and steam whistling from between the wheel's teeth; far forward some men in blue uniforms are loading frozen cardboard boxes onto the dining car. The moment of leaving seems to stretch itself like a celestial synthetic. Who was that man?

ROYAL FLUSH

The signs say *Ne flushez pas le toilette quand le tren est standing en gare if you don't want to get in real trouble, comprenez?* or something like that, her French is high school; but she *always* forgets and she's flushed it anyhow. What can she say? Shout "Sorry!!" out the window?

Were these the secrets that Cary Grant and Eva Marie Saint knew and never told us about? The oddities of traveling by train across a bilingual continent. It happened one night. Outside her window sixty pronghorn antelope go springing across a yellow-and-white world, printing and printing with their tiny hooves the perpetual message of endangered species, like hearts, the words: *Honey, you're going to miss me when I'm gone.*

LETTER

She writes a letter, not to be mailed, but to create a second person singular, a "You." She is inventing somebody to take the place of an absence, to whom she can leave all the agency, where she can place all the blame. She doesn't know that "You" is the most dangerous address in the universe. Just listen:

"I used to wake up from these horrible dreams and you would be there, I used to struggle to bring us both out of our separate sleeps so that you could comfort me. I used to swim and swim toward the surface—it was always up there somewhere—I wanted so badly to be rescued and you were always rescuing everybody but me.

"I'll meet you there in Montreal and we will go to Les Filles du Roi and have the most unbelievable food, and we will look at each other across the table, through all that candlelight and its colors of banana and gilt and then we will get into an argument about who's paying for the dinner! *You're* paying for it, and for another dinner if I want it, and another one after that, and if you ask what my life has meant to me so far, I'll tell you that not only do I want to be loved, but I want to be rich. So drop dead."

Oh what a character I have invented, she thinks, putting down her Parker. The pillbox hat with the little veil is lying on the chair. She's looking out at the last of the Bow River and all those earth-and-redwood-colored condos just outside of Calgary that look like desert camouflage bunkers, and thinks: *nobody can get me on the phone or otherwise.*

TRANSITION

The train is a universe that moves and jangles through a perfectly still landscape, creating apparent storms, a tunnel of shakes, a dimension of crackerjack efficiencies. The cook sharpens his long knives in the kitchen dining car with steely crashing noises, and the meat he is about to slice lies quivering on the counter; helpless and appalled. You can look up from your dinner and see the Cypress Hills, bald and blue, like friendly and curious asteroids peeking up just above the horizon that might at any moment turn feral and start to attack. Because of this she suggests they go back to the lounge car and read magazines; it will be something they can do with their minds. The mind goes ticking forward through the time of our lives as long as its gears are engaged; hers is at present occupied by the armies of guilt and regret and who's going to claim the babies?

GETTING YOURSELF TOGETHER

She knows it's very important *exactly* how the lips are shaped, width of hips and color of eyes. She sits in front of the triple mirrors over the dressing table and checks it out; she's always checking it out. It is as if she were personally responsible before the presumed male observer for every jointure and color, as if she has put herself together single-handedly, as if she had bought herself at a big downtown Seattle store, charged herself on a credit card—probably at the cosmetics counter, Estee Lauder—watching with satisfaction and a sense of fury and courage as the metal imprinter, like a miniature rolling mill creating her presence out of cosmetics, mink, and plastic cash, racketed across the gold-and-blue card: *crash crash* and there you are! A nose, eyes, you got it, the whole manufactured face, the body beautifully designed. Outside, Alberta is sliding off toward a province called *Saskatchewan*; she's not even sure how to pronounce it. Her adventurousness has outrun her fund of general knowledge. The train jumps sideways and her eyeliner runs a long streak up her temple. *Watch it!* She was thinking about The Man from China Bar. *I want somebody to look into my eyes and want me. I want somebody to choose me and nobody else but me out of a crowd of people, out of all these passengers on this train, a man to walk into my life big as destiny and purpose, out of all these people on this train.*

Scarlett, Rhett, and a cast of thousands.

Am I beautiful? Almost beautiful? Not beautiful enough?

FLASHBACK: THE BACKGROUND

She surrounded herself with the right images: travel calendars, framed posters, can't get enough of those contemporary novels (*The Pill Dolls* and *Dying for Some*); she read *Esquire* to catch up on what the New Man is thinking about: money, sometimes. Women. *I want to stay at the Lancaster in Paris, which epitomizes the discreet wealth and good manners of its setting on the Right Bank, but I don't want to stay at a replica of the Lancaster in brash Houston or Dallas, as that Texas millionairess would have me do. An instructive example, again, is Haiti. Despite its position on a hill at the end of a drive, the ramshackle Oloffson embraces the colorful squalor outside its gates.* Hotels. The New Man is thinking about hotels and colorful squalor. If you get up in the morning and read this while you have your coffee, it will make you shiny.

She works in a low-grade job at a Seattle television news station; her friends are all pissed off at her—"*She's in such a terrible mood these days,*" they say, and ram pushpins through heads of state. Taking the bus home at night, wearing pink plastic Chinese shoes, she can see whole sections of Seattle laid out, and the lights in the median darkness and drifting rain show up her face in the bus window, her terrible energy shining out like the teeth of Lucifer. The lost temper: where do tempers go when you lose them? Her ideas don't have any whole connections, they fall out in sections and terraces like Japanese land usage. When they all go to the bar after work, she thinks, *Wanda's not talking to me, she's afraid I'll start in on that Japanese land usage thing. But it was a good story idea, I know it was. But researchers aren't supposed to have good story ideas, we're supposed to research.* She should get on a train and go somewhere—the Orient Express, the Trans-Siberian—like Vanessa Redgrave or Vivien Leigh, maybe up in Canada across the Rockies. And then get into a fast skid of invention, all the people and colorful squalor she ever wanted to invent. Offices! Offices! Thousands of women in offices! With a grade twelve education she'll be here forever; the only way she could be more stuck is if she had two grade twelve educations. City College anybody? Life is really 60–40 at this point, flipping furiously through the newspaper files looking for something. A head of state. She wants to know how to perform with grace under stress, like Butterfly McQueen or Mae West. If only she had less debt, more money, more grace, less stress. Shirley and Wanda review their personality amputations with pride. "I used to want to," says Shirley. "But now I realize that." Wanda confesses that she "used to think you could" and laughs over her coffee, "Ha ha isn't that just the way you think when you're a teenager? You think the world's your . . . you know what." They have put so much effort into acquiring new and better personalities; she regards them with rage, crushing Lifesavers between her cute teeth.

AQUARIUS

Travel is favored if you keep a tight lid on expenditures, but don't let the cat out of the bag, especially concerning career interests. Romance and leisure activities will be fulfilling if you just don't let the cat out of the bag.

YOU BORN TODAY remember you may not get born again so lucky; maybe next time in the middle of a war. At times bouts of temperament can throw you off balance, for you're high-strung and can sometimes be observed throwing the office potted plants out the fourth-story window. Travel is favored if you can buy all the tickets on credit cards. Birthday of: Paulette Goddard, Franchot Tone, Irwin Shaw.

Shirley and Wanda and Our Heroine go to the bar after work, and Our Heroine practices what she thinks of as her new bland personality. It seems to please everybody, including one of the reporters she's been trying to get a date with. Seeing this, appalled by its success, she gets up and leaves, goes directly to a travel agency and buys as many train tickets as she can in the shortest amount of time on every credit card she possesses. She will keep going. She will purchase a set of matched luggage and a fur coat. She's going to run up debts of third world proportions and what can they do about it? She'll be in Canada on a train. She's going to feel what it's like to be rich and not care what people think of you. Ever. To be totally graceless under stress, to be outrageous, to talk about any idea she wants to, to walk out of the world in a trail of fire.

TREE SHADOWS

She hopes we are inhabited by a soul, fired with purpose as an engine is fired with coal in a boiler. Oh look at the old days, and how they used to jive, and at what speed, and under what steams! The mystery is jumping in and out of these dimensions; and flying behind us as we emerge comes railroad silver, and pink plastic Chinese slippers, a knight in shining armor, French dictionaries, breakfast buns, the Three Wise Men, hair straightener, Hawaiian shell necklaces, Filipino coins and books like these, books on old trains with old photographs giving the names and numbers of the steam engines. They seem, like dinosaurs, about to sink into a sepia earth. She flips the page, a running series of tree shadows flies past the dining car windows like a girl running a stick down a picket fence.

"I just picked it up in Vancouver at the train station," he says. "Something to read."

"But you got on at China Bar."

"That's right, I did, but I . . ." and in those three dots lie many hidden purposes!

He's a son-of-a-gun with adventures in every pocket.

LATER

Our Heroine is playing a three-way game of Canasta in the bar, absorbed; she has to be engaged in something, the way vamps and butlers are always somewhere else when the action happens. He excuses himself and walks up the aisle and without furtiveness into Compartment C. He begins to go quickly and efficiently through her luggage. The most important is the zipper case where she keeps her identification cards, and he goes through them one after the other, noting at least three different names (listening all the time for possible footsteps in the corridor), looking at the dates and destinations on her amazing collection of train tickets (Jesus Christ, she's the Flying Dutchman), looking at matchbook covers (names of restaurants and motels, all of them either Seattle or Vancouver), labels on clothing (here is a stapled-on dayglo tag—definitely Salvation Army), running the edges of a thick diary against his thumb and several sheets of self-reflections, which of course contain nothing more than imprecations against people named Shirley and Wanda—as if typewriter fonts would do him any good—opening her makeup bag, reading the labels on medicine bottles, the dates and names of doctors and pharmacies (all Seattle), then putting it all back. There's an antique change purse with a fifty-drachma note, and then he goes through the credit cards with a sinking heart, realizing with horror—the dread that Percival never knew—that the object of pursuit was indeed within reach. Seven credit cards, in three different names, and only one of them her real and hidden name, which he assumes is the same name on the army-green American passport, recently acquired, and no stamps on it yet. Which means she has no intention of returning to the United States from Canada, and his mind runs out on the strands of a web of possibilities. Europe, Mexico, Greece, but probably not China. Her paperback novels are all in English; they have pictures of rich and beautiful women on the front. Her appointment book (leather binding, recently acquired, unused—like the mink coat, the shoes, the gold jewelry—she seems to have created herself out of credit cards) has no appointments. There are no tropical-weight clothes and no rain-coats. Compartment C is a treasure house of hot items. He looks up at the unopenable window and considers chucking it all out and sug-gesting *Start all over.* They are passing a freight going the other way and the bars of sunshine, light-pulses, flash between the coal cars and the grain cars. He gazes at it for a moment, hypnotized by the Doppler effect of the screaming whistle.

Yes, there really is a body on this car.

REACHING FOR FIRE

They are nearly to the Saskatchewan border; the evening is blue and shaky. He watches her play Canasta and wonders if he can hear his watch tick even in this train noise. *I could just quit the job; that's one option.* He would like to have a different history and become somebody else, but he feels things like magazine advertisements press-ing him into one simple persona. He was supposed to have been an investigator of fraud, and fraud has always intrigued him, fraud and those who employ fraud as a device to obtain food, clothing, shelter, adventure, and a background. Their apparent fronts, like stage sets, designed to tell a charming and simple *fable.* But she is beginning to unnerve him; he's dropping things—his package of cigarettes, his matches—sitting across from her. He watches the bartender drift by on salary. The train is pulling him forward like a zipper and he's opening up; some idea, unnerving and eastbound, is unbuttoning it-self. He doesn't like the way he sees thoughts moving in her, hard as little glaciers. She has the innocent and spontaneous savagery of the starved, in I. Miller shoes, and he can't even guess the label on the suit. Is it possible he has always shared the world with people like this? Maybe she's not seeing herself through his eyes! Will he have to share the visual field? He wants to reach across the intervening space and seize her wrist like Paleolithic man reaching for fire. *Come on and let's get out of the whole system.* After all, she hasn't embezzled anything. She hasn't held up a bank, not yet anyway. This isn't *Guns at Cyrano's.* She's guarded behind her glossy contemporary stereotype; she's loving every minute of being encased in that flashy binding like a book somebody is giving a big sell. He wants her to come out of the character she's playing. *Will you come out of there,* he would say to her, *and give me a straight answer?* (There is no straight answer.) But the story of his pursuit is becoming so compelling that he can't remember his ending. (There is no ending.) He thinks, only briefly, about being poor, and female. What if waiters no longer spoke to him in respectful, quiet tones; what if women no longer gave him way on the street but crowded him instead; what if nobody made up his bed, typed his letters, didn't look away but stared at or through him? He watches her as she shuffles the deck, dealing cards to the Americans from Houston and New Orleans. *I could take it,* he tells himself. *I'm so tough I can tear matchbooks in half.* He tears a matchbook in half; well, she's not so fucking poor any longer, is she? He imagines himself interrogating her, relentlessly. *What's it like?* She will tell him, he knows, the absolute truth, starting with the small details.

FIRST CLASS

This is the great unknown unspoken secret of North America: ladies don't work, women do. She doesn't have to talk about her job because interesting ladies don't have jobs. They have *interests.* She's read enough contemporary novels to pass for class. Men give her appreciative glances, especially with the mink, and she imagines she looks like a studio portrait of Gene Tierney and maybe she does. The man who got on at China Bar for instance. He's asking her about *herself.* Which is flattering and also makes her nervous. Imagine that clammy little reporter back at the television station, allowing her to sit beside him, interrupting her in mid-sentence without even saying excuse me, expecting her to nod appreciatively at his interruption; what crapola. It's late and towns are going past them like displays. He takes her hand and looks at the diamond-and-sapphire ring, runs his thumb over the inside fire and draws it out into his hand, where he seems to have put it in his waistcoat pocket.

She looks down at the ring. It is empty. Its deep iridescence glows fiercely in the dark of his waistcoat.

"That's an amazing ring."

"I found it between the seats of a Greyhound bus."

"Going where?"

"To meet somebody. My friend. Last week, in Spokane. The man I'm seeing."

"Shit." He leans back in his chair and laughs. "Shit."

FAIRY TALES

She ends up talking to him late at night in the club car, even though she knows she should not be talking to anybody late at night in the club car, so in order to both please and avoid giving information she lies, as usual.

"I'm from Montreal," she says. "Oh well, no I'm not. Not really. I'm not really from Montreal but I'm going to Montreal." And she says, "I'm just *going* to Montreal. I'm from Seattle. And in Seattle . . . well, I've quit my job. I mean, my interests. I got fed up with all my interests. You didn't really shoot the Fraser Canyon in a Volvo, did you? What does that mean, shooting a river? I quit my work and I feel terrible about it. Well, no, really, I didn't quit work. I got fired.

"I got fired and it was horrible; I hate getting fired. I was a producer. This is the third time I've been fired in my entire life. And I've got family in St. Louis and I might go there if I want to. There's a restaurant there on the levee, it's a wonderful place, and I might go there from Montreal if I felt like it. If I had a train ticket I'd go there."

And she s-t-a-n-d-s up and smashes out her cigarette as if she were following stage directions.

ESCAPE PLANS

She knew she would meet a man on the train. It's part of the script. Of course there are men on trains every day all over the continent. But.

She gets out the diagrams showing the layout of the Park cars, the dining car, the baggage and the coaches. How can we compartmentalize our lives, and everything? Are these things really blueprints which assure us that nothing surprising will ever happen? Searching the diagrams carefully, we see that there are no people in them, only places for people. Coach seats and lounge chairs, little tables in the bar cars, the fold-out beds in the sleeping cars and the dressing tables, toilets, mirrors—there is something Pompeian about this, this empty ghostly train making its black-and-white way across Canada. A train made of diagrams, where specters experience only the predicted experiences, think the fashionable thoughts of their generation of specters.

It is evening. Small beautiful things are happening overhead like stars. There isn't anything yet empty or wanting. She doesn't want him yet, and so nothing is spoiled. The Americans have fallen into novels and newspapers. She searches the diagrams, not for reassurance, but in case she would want to escape, hide, leap off the train.

A RESERVATION FOR TWO

But here's the real horror story: she will have survived the nightmares and Kicking Horse Pass, the murder in the club car, the waiter, and arrived in Montreal; and she would have met him or somebody, and they will have gone to Les Filles du Roi and all its atmospherics in a taxi, and ordered dinner, only to find that she has been served *imitation crab* made out of pollock and fish cheeks! How can you ever know what you're getting? It's a question of money and its total lack of interest in the real thing; only prices. Maybe she'd better be happy she made it across Canada without being located by skip-tracers; that she has something to eat at all.

CHEATING AT CARDS

He is almost angry that she would be like this, out of the rigid images of dry reports, or that his pursuit would become so reluctant, almost as if he were the one pursued. She could well rise in the night and get off at some prairie station, some tiny, remote galaxy of lights that would then disappear into the firmament of wheat. Maybe it wasn't her. And if it isn't her, of course, then it's somebody else. They are playing ninety-nine, his fingers feel thick and inaccurate as he deals the deck between them.

"Tell me about doing the sound for that Australian movie," she says.

"It's complicated."

"Well, tell me the first thing you did when you went to work in the morning." She drops a one-eyed jack on him. "Jump-back jack."

"I walked up to Tina Turner, kissed her passionately, and then we had big danishes."

"What a job."

"There it is. Tell me the first thing you do when you go to work in the morning."

She remembers just in time she's a railroad detective.

"I walk into the Amtrak office and look around for the biggest man. I pick a guy and say, 'Come with me.' And we dress up in old clothes and go down to the rail yards and we start looking for hoboes. Sometimes we just ride around with the hoboes. We look for *clues*."

The Man held up all the face cards he had: a queen of spades, a king of diamonds, a jack of hearts.

"You know, sweetheart, someday you're going to have to tell all these nice people the truth."

LOVE SCENE

Our Heroine is lying on the bed in her compartment, lonesome and subdued. The door opens. Enter Man from China Bar.

"I thought you might want some peanuts. They have wonderful peanuts on the train here in Canada."

"I had some peanuts."

"I thought you also might like this drink."

"I had too many already."

"It was an excuse to come into your compartment."

"Last time it was coffee. You're a regular catering service."

"Take the goddamn drink, will you?"

"I love masterful men."

Our Heroine takes the drink and sets it on the dressing table as if it were full of nitroglycerine. THE MAN FROM CHINA BAR moves stage left and sits on the bed.

"Have you noticed the enormous sexual energy generated on trains?"

"Yes, yes I have and it gives me goose pimples. Look at my arm."

THE MAN FROM CHINA BAR takes her arm and draws her down onto the bed. He tells himself to slow down. He slows down. She slows down. He feels like speeding up again and as a matter of interest wonders if she travels around picking up men on trains. Not for the last two months, at least, he's sure of that, but anyway, in general. They kiss; it's Twentieth Century Fox.

POINT OF VIEW

They begin to emerge out of the matrix of major stereotypes. They could have been symbols of anything: of male and female, of Canada and the United States, of refinement versus the untutored, of upper class and working class, child and adult, *sauvage* and urban. They could also be clichés of America's view of Canada as nothing but landscape. Of Canada's view of Americans as people who indulge in exotic squalor and high-rolling. They could be light and dark, love and hate, pursuit and flight, or approach and avoidance. They move into the hot sexual ambushes of the dark. The story is about some-body's body lying all along yours, somebody's mouth very close to your ear so that even the smallest whisper or intake of breath is heard clearly. Whisper of cloth, or no cloth.

FLOWERS ON A DARK BACKGROUND

She puts her arms around him and is afraid, briefly, that he will put his hands around her throat. And she is afraid he will wrap his hand around her arm above the elbow hard enough to bruise it. And she is afraid they might remember who they were before they took their clothes off.

They are crossing borders in the night they did not even realize they had; moving into strange provinces, unconscious and alone beside one another in sleep, major and minor arcana, in their dreams, in their solitude—where in the territory of earth are they now—if at all?

SILK TRAIN

Trains move down wholesale on entire towns, running across complete landscapes, under the tall fantasies of farmers' clouds which refinish themselves each mile they move forward toward the other end of this place.

He finds himself plunging forward like a train, heavily, on a prescribed and circumscribed route, with intent; impressing himself on every landscape that arrives. It all has to be dealt with and catalogued, grasped quickly and then thrown behind him before something new arrives; something even more threatening. Little ties whipping by as if somebody were riffling the cards of a wooden deck, and for some reason neither one of them can let go without fear of being

Swept Away.

He has been imprinting himself on the world, making promises to arrive at stations at the right time, a man turns around only to find somebody has punched a hole in his ticket (It's a dirty job etc.) and does this mean he's no good anymore? He hurries forward toward Montreal with a name and an address he could swear to in court, unlike her, as if Montreal were the Last Judgment and he were sure it was going to be in his favor.

MASTER CONTROL

They woke up still barely west of Regina. They looked out and saw antelopes fleeing like agile burglars, surprised in a cactus robbery.

They are still sleepy, tangled in the thin old Canadian Pacific sheets, and the light woolen blankets. They almost feel like captured bandits being transported across this existence to some vast, metropolitan dimension of another life, heavy with stolen gold. As if they were captured but about to escape out of their stereotypes, stripping free, betraying their employers, their Master Control, rebelling, blowing their contracts.

He is not who she thinks he is. He has a history, an ex-wife, a grammar school record, moments of which he is ashamed, memories of embarrassment and fear; he has habits, his knees, his socks, his obligations.

He sits up and pushes up the blind, his hand on her instep.

He says, "Where the hell are we?" and "Jesus Christ, are you smoking already?"

It's so hard to fall in love! It's harder not to fall in love. By this time they are coming toward Regina blowing a whistle, and the Americans have sat up with their game all night and apparently murdered somebody; not anybody you would want to know. (Probably another American; they are caught between violence and repentance; which do you want?)

MOVING ON THE MARGINS

The Man from China Bar comes down the length of the sleeping cars carrying coffee, "excuse me, excuse me." He can't imagine why he got into this dalliance, especially with a suspect. He can't imagine now why he ever took the job, running down the illegally rich, the borderline, the demented people who can't resist advertising, the ones who are addicted to the sound of the charge card's little printing press. "Excuse me." People who are moved by the gigantic images on movie screens, where everybody lives in an interesting tangle of problems; like his, and risk only their lives and not their money; like her. "Excuse me." Except people like this are just so much more interesting; he wants to find out what it's like when you're making up your own story, when you're not the center of a precast myth, when nobody gives you deference and you do it single-handed. It's a dirty job but somebody's got to do it. Moving on the margins, a skip-tracer. "Excuse me, sorry."

RULES OF THE GAME

The porter, full of stiff disapproval, has already made up the compartment and they sit, drinking coffee, watching the arrival of landscape. He takes out his pen and notebook and decides to make up his own rules.

Rules for Operatives
in the Canadian Ajax Skip-Tracer Agency

1. Take local transportation when possible and charge it.
2. Remember everything you come across, and where it was put last, especially food, women, and bills of large denomination.
3. Write down vital signs in your notebook.
4. Drink whiskey.
5. Get up front to the engine once in a while to see how Fate is running your life.
6. Never drink whiskey on Wednesdays.
7. Dream dreams and write them down the next morning and interpret them the following night and stay away from other people's compartments, especially those of women suspects who glance at you over their magazines in the club car.
8. Dreams have reasons which are usually listed under number 9; they are thought out at the center of the earth, and then played out here, on the surface, in the red stone slot of the Fraser, in the north's blue snows, across sea-tone prairies; the armature of dreams and their strange vocabularies.
9. Fill in the blanks.

REPETITION

Early morning; they approach the city of Winnipeg. After this? Europe, maybe, or Mexico. How would she get there? She'd go there and freelance news or something; maybe help all those hot shit reporters from the television news teams. She's a good researcher. How do you think she figured out the credit card scam? Researchers know strange things. She looks at him leaning back in the lounge armchair, a magazine on his lap, coffee; he's gazing out at the prairie and its lengthy silks running westward and yellow. His interesting large beaky nose and soiled tie, a scratchy morning shave and all the flat, two-dimensional images of sex and presence that people stand in front of them like enormous flexible paper dolls. She wonders if she's starting to get fed up: with being sober and being drunk, sick of being cool and tall and smart, tired of little pillbox hats with veils; she's tired of trains and yet she can't get off. It just keeps happening over and over, it just keeps happening over and over.

THE HUDSON'S BAY COMPANY

Winnipeg. They had an hour to walk down to Portage and Main where humanity, in a long procession, moves slowly out of the archives of the Hudson's Bay Company and disappears into postmodern slums. The factors, the Cree captains, the man who almost died at the long portage of the Sturgeon River, the man who wrote from the Hudson Bay Coast in 1679, "Snowing, blowing, shot a crow with one ball flying," a minimalist.

I could leave the train right now and dump this sleazoid, she thinks and wonders where would be the best place to hide; *maybe he's a skiptracer.* She is getting more nervous. She could disappear into a department store, pose as a dress dummy as he runs around the cosmetics counters of Eaton's or Simpson's or The Bay; *she's slipped out of our grasp, lieutenant. Again.* Or she is caught; she would claim she'd never done anything like this before in her life. They'd let her off; *go straight, young woman.* But they happen to be strolling back toward the train station. It's Montreal or nothing.

Maybe they'll have caught up with her here. She's restless, waiting for the train to move, hiding in her compartment. At this point there is nothing anybody can do but go forward and prepare themselves for what might come; the bald geography of prairies and the night.

From now on she only has one road: it is like a New Year's resolution; simple and full of traps.

DETECTIVE FICTION

Well, it's a kind of minor form; a sly genre in which the subject of class is taken on and in which something has to be arranged for the pursuit and capture of a desired object.

Why do you have to have a plot at all? Why not, as in legends, simply slide your characters forward on the smooth surface of gigantic contradictions, moving them forward as if on a train, placing each one carefully in correct clothes like paper dolls; the sex scenes are the ones in which the clothes fall off of them, if you remember playing with paper dolls. And how hard it was to keep the clothes on them; the pulp and paper romances you invented. You give them each a motivation, which will lead to the necessity of taking action; you construct the relationship, the background, the scenes of sex or intimacy or both (sunlight in rectangles falling through the compartment window on skin and lace and his cheap polyester tie in the sink, with flamingos on it), protagonists holding each other or their representatives (see my lawyer), her thighs open to him, his hand on her back. They grasp each other's images, which will return like paper dolls to the printed page in the morning.

The train is locked into a rigid schedule of train time, a series of halts and marches. And now Our Heroine and The Man from China Bar read magazines; they talk in small, cautious sentences, commenting on the landscape. They could really give a big shit about the landscape. The bartender in his blue jacket regards them (another train romance) quietly above the elbow of his sunken bar behind the 1950s etched and frosted glass, arranging his scotch, his wines, his rum both dark and light, and the high-pressure bottle of Karma-Kola. *Another train romance.* He watches them turn to each other, forming profiles. He passes by them with a tray of drinks and coffee (the American tour group is unfolding its characters again, all of whom are single-minded) and hears the low-tone laughter of Our Heroine and The Man from China Bar; a dialogue of whispers and jokes. It looks like they will be gliding into snow on the other side of Sudbury, tall bearded columns of descending frost. What really happens with train romances, detective novels, pursuit and flight? In these situations, does one really live only in the present instant? If so, we remain within the confines of the lyric, and if it goes on, then we have a plot, which makes a story. He said, she said, and who shot John. The bartender wonders who the story really belongs to—to himself, the marginal observer who is so dignified and deferential that nobody even notices his deference; to the porters, who make up beds; to the women on the train who support the work of conversations without even knowing they're doing it; or the white men who seem to be locked in privilege—or if a story is property at all and can be owned? The bartender is reticent and Jamaican, and so nobody has inquired enough to know that his mind is a sailboat made of magical disturbances, like all minds; and it is sailing sideways through the moving universe under a Genoa jib and full main. But the Americans want him to be The Butler again in their endless game of Clue, and again Mr. Boddy falters and dies, and again the vamps, the rich widows, the alcoholic uncles, the knives and lead pipes come into play as if they made a story merely by being there. The train moves eastward. The Man from China Bar listens to Our Heroine, who is talking about imaginary restaurants in Montreal; he is watching the faint, almost-snowing light on her hair and cheek, and her shoulders inside that swank silk blouse, for which, he knows, she has not yet paid.

COMING OUT OF IT

The trees begin in eastern Manitoba in long fingers of spruce, as if the jointure of prairie and the forest country had folded its hands together and were sitting in church, listening to a Protestant sermon on the sins of that madman, Louis Riel. Through it all the train, with its architecture of speed, a housing of transient and expectant souls, crashes eastward. The stiff joints of the blue Canadian Pacific cars bend around the rare and remarkable curves. The train is throwing itself and its passengers recklessly into the rapid visual noise of the boreal rebellion, and the Lac Seul magic of Ojibway revenge which is so sweet that passengers shooting through the town of Hudson fast

as a World War II silk train think they have been blessed with a brief
and strange perfume, like people being sprayed with testers at a cosmetics counter, and they only find out later.

The nature of absolute truth is that it is too boring to endure
without a frontal lobotomy, and there is for most of us no virtue in it
anyhow; and the universe is not putting out any daily editions that
we can understand, and here's the *Regina Leader-Post* among all the
magazines and dailies in the lounge car—a blue little prairie gazette,
but what can you do? With its subtle Saskatchewan heart.

Truth is an absolute concept thought up after the invention of
protracted and deliberate lying, which came shortly after the invention, not of speech, but of grammar. She reads the newspapers from
Canada's major cities back in the lounge car. She considers taking up
white-collar crime to take care of her debts, white-collar crime being
the single lifetime adventure of accountants—double entries are their
way of shooting rapids and smoking Camels—but she decides against
it. She'd have to get a white-collar job again, and having an affair on
a train isn't the way to go about that. Should she be an *adventuress?*
She shakes out the *Thunder Bay Times-News. Adventuress,* she thinks,
remembering Paulette Goddard playing some exotic Métis character
named Yvette with a knife in her teeth, who was rescued by a Mountie, the Mountie dressed in vast tentlike furs with tails of things
hanging off all over him. *Adventuress, I love that word.* She looks out
the lounge car window; the train is racing south. *It goes with my hat.*
The train thinks up more steam to say to the world like a smartass
comment, speeding around the solid granite mountains of the North
Shore, full of backchat and passengers. Ooooooooooooooeeeeeeeee, you
can imagine it saying. Do your own sound track for this one. Do
yourself a Doppler and imagine it, steam and all.

Of course you can tell the truth. Like a Girl Scout swearing on
a tiny Bible, you just tell what you saw, an honest witness to the

world's five-car pileup; you tell either what you saw or what happened to you, in sequence, in color, in all honesty. Make yourself look good. Never mind the jury sitting here around the club car who have already been instructed by the bartender on the unreliability of eyewitnesses, even if you are being the eyewitness to your own life, or at least several aspects of your own life and all its dancing in ruby shoes (or what you think are ruby shoes). Or at least, you're doing the best you can. Or at least, well, bartender, bring me another rum and Karma-Kola. Tonight is my night. I'm going to go down to the *voiture-restaurant* and take my false self out to dinner and buy it anything it wants.

The train goes pelting through the darkness of the great lake shores, and her face shows up in the other side of the window glass. The dark side. It wasn't a lover as much as a job. She got fired from a Seattle television station and decided to go to Vancouver and take a train trip across the country: someplace you could take liberties with reality, shore leave with the hard facts, running like a blind person over the braille of Alberta's cryptic geography and the Canadian Shield and its several moons: the Oil Moon and the North Moon and the Blue Moons of Unemployment. The train charges down the tracks into the blackening happy night, down the typeface of the double rails and ties, as if it were a typewriter carriage engaged upon an endless sentence—all of it in upper case, all of it in Helvetica Bold 48-point—typing out, like a transcontinental court reporter, the truth, the whole truth, and nothing but the truth.

ZEN AND THE ART OF TRAIN TRAVEL

The Man from China Bar looks out at the twisted, torn, ripped sheet metal sticking up into the air like the freeze-dried flags of a robot army; a derailed freight.

Nothing is safe. Anything that has forward momentum is at risk; and like all your years behind you the freights, with all that weight and tonnage, are strung out on lines of temporality. What is to stop it? Ever? The Man from China Bar thinks how if anything were to bring him to a halt now how his entire life would pile up behind him and jackknife; he would catch fire; all those moments of passion being

immense loads, like the year 1976. It would simply catapult right off
the tracks. But he couldn't have lived without 1976, either.

They lie on their stomachs, smoking, watching out the frozen-
over sill of the train window, watching the slow, lovely arrival of
white lights in the distant towns presented by the horizon again and
again, as if they had been turned on like theaters for their arrival.

"When we were in France," she says. "When I was eight."

"I thought you grew up poor in Missouri," he whispers suspi-
ciously into her hair.

"Oh, that was a lie, I made that up. No, actually, I didn't. I have
a friend who told me that. About her aunt and the feather ticks. And
so I told it like it was me."

"So tell me a story about France."

"They have terrible cigarettes in France. The kind like we smoke
are expensive."

"So you were smoking in France when you were eight years old."

"You've got to stop not believing me."

"I believe you. Right now I believe you."

They rush forward into all that naked geography. They hear the
porter walking down the hall outside. It's one-thirty and almost everybody has gone to sleep except themselves; they are now in total possession of the train—they and the Americans, who are desperately
trying to find out if it was Lauren Bacall, in the Caribbean.

SHE THINKS

I don't have to show anybody what love is; everybody should figure
it out for themselves. Women are always going around showing men
what "love" is, the way the moon shows Easter Week how to get out
of April (straight through the almanac's corridor); we're supposed to
guide and seduce them, open their fists into hands, and is it worth
it? My own brain is in a fist half the time anyway; is it worth spending

your whole life doing this? She thinks of him, without a guide, lost in the dense prose jungles of *She* and making squishing noises in the rain forest telephone booth where he is trying to dial MACHINE and BRUTE STRENGTH and WEAPON and CRUSH, or is he really? Maybe he thinks she would dial CLING and BLAME and MANIPULATE. Well, just let him! Look, look, he finally makes it out by dialing CIVILIZATION, with his heart in his left hand like a valentine, and herself on the train, rocketing toward Monday and November and Montreal. She lights up a cigarillo, blowing the tobacco fumes toward him, smoky and seductive as Chicago.

LAKE SUPERIOR

The train has long windows that weep with frost all the way around the north shore of Lake Superior. The train is a perpetual performance, a carnival, a traveling medicine show, a sort of genteel psych ward going around the bend. Far ahead you can see the engine, running very fast, following its own light like a soul being preceded through the gates of heaven or hell by the ferryman. We have come through Hell's Gate, haven't we? Well then. Down the aisles the porter steps on his crepe soles, with his flashlight shining, looking for strays; or for rents in the fabric of this moving universe, through which other porters enquire, with flashlights even more luminous than his. Occasionally he finds them.

THE THIRD NIGHT

They sit in his compartment, evening of the third night, they pass through the nameless villages of the Shield Country and the spruce standing endlessly to attention: the trinity of Church and Train Station and The Hudson's Bay with their lonely hard-rock night lights; and as in a stage set, everything is brief, perfect and understandable in one quick glance. In one town a group of people stand knee-deep in the harsh pool of station lights, grouped around a police car for some unknown reason, staring at the passing train with a disembodied expectancy that makes The Man from China Bar and Our Heroine almost feel *seen* or *waited for* by an audience or a reader waiting for their plots to unfold, and the people at the station, like restless observers, saying *do something.* Then they have flown past—one of the women standing by the police car was holding a white duck.

OPENING THE DOOR TO STRANGERS

She thinks about some kind of question to ask him; about himself. Men are such suckers for questions about themselves; and if you talk about your own thoughts they always interrupt you and so, like, don't fight it. To avoid having anything serious to do with this situation she thinks about some kind of interested comment to make on his naked rib cage and she runs her fingers down his shoulder and arm. And if she has to say something about herself it will be something that makes her appear *absolutely normal and bland.* It will be a lie.

It will be something she either imagined or read in a book. She can't believe he's actually asking her questions about herself. But, of course, this is why detective fiction is as it is. In it, impossible things happen, like this one. She wonders why the hell she invited him into Compartment C. But haven't we all, at some time in our lives, voluntarily opened our compartments to strange visitors, wanting and yet not wanting, tempted and afraid? The train is really moving now, toward Sudbury and its acid rock. He wants to know about her shares in the Seattle television station and there's nothing to do but invent something.

WHICH BODY?

And so she says, "Did you *ever* smoke?"

Because she's depending on the fact that men like to talk about themselves, and can always be deflected from unpleasant reality by same, and that he will tell her how he used to smoke, and how he quit, and how hard it was, and the way he figured out not to smoke, and he will give her advice on how not to smoke herself. This is only their second night together; maybe the last.

Her ashes fall on the Canadian Pacific sheets and she blows them away, like her feelings. And the pleasant, repetitive rhythm of passenger trains occurs and occurs, the feeling of violent forward movement. Moving into the future, the past strung out far behind across the continent like train smoke; but whose past was it, anyway?

"No, I never did."

She's got to look around for something else. "Are the Americans back there still playing Clue?"

"Yeah. And guess who joined them? An exotic dancer, she says she's going to Montreal and she's traveling with her pet snake. It's up in the baggage car."

"Oh gak!! You mean I'm traveling with a Canadian snake all the way to Montreal?"

"Which is worse: the snake or an imaginary body?"

"Depends," she says. She reaches over and strokes his stomach with all its hair. "Which body."

EXPLORERS

He starts to try to explain everything to her.

"Look, there are such things as alternative universes. The one right next to us is extremely dull. It's called Blandworld. The people in it are worried if they're good enough for whatever, and the thing that keeps their universe going is that they never are. The world runs on the electricity of anxiety. I was a long, bulky yacht in my father's marina, and one day the anxiety wore through my lines and I just broke loose. I've been drifting ever since."

"Being a sound tekkie on major films doesn't sound like drifting to me."

"Yeah, right." He has almost forgotten his story.

HOLOGRAMS ON PARADE

She knows he is, in some way, moving in on her, so she becomes even more evasive by kissing him. She offers a false image. Maybe he'll be content with it; maybe he'll think it's the real thing. Meanwhile, like an animal discarding a leg in a trap, she'll become the mink she's wearing and disappear into the snow. She'll gather up her tracks behind her like glittering frozen bread crumbs. "What's the matter?" he says, holding her back. She is beginning to waver in and out of vision, like print when your eyes are tired. He's trying to remember when he learned that this sort of invitation, this sweetness, was an evasion. And he wants it at the same time. "I'm having a great time," he says. "Wish you were here." That's right. It was a postcard from the last person he didn't quite catch up with. A postcard with a raving beauty on the front. The postcard was from Peru. It said, *Bang*. A hot shot.

SHE CHANGES THE RULES

While he is gone for coffee she goes swiftly and efficiently through his luggage, looking for who he *really* is. She finds a shaving kit with shaving stuff in it, all grotty with hairs, and matchbooks from all over the place. Maybe the train made him up, maybe the train supplied him with matchbooks from all the major cities of Canada. To be invented by a train! And his papers with an expense account (he was claiming all that rum and Karma-Kola; what a cheapskate!) Also a clothing catalogue called *Cockpit* which advertised a lot of World-War II flying jackets—good god, here's the Vintage "Raider" Jacket: "Clark Gable wore one in the 1939 epic Test Pilot, flying Spencer Tracy's race-equipped P35, and Harrison Ford wore a twin in Raiders . . . special vintage effect of aged, timeworn leather in a completely new, handcrafted jacket." There you are; the guy's a loony. Or, maybe, a fellow loony. Searching through somebody's possessions in Compartment D is a low-grade occupation and she's properly ashamed of herself but a full-time criminal can't be too careful. All his clothing labels are from one tailor in Victoria; that's taste. At least he hasn't got a Raider jacket. Although he must have been tempted. She checked the catalogue again. Actually the price wasn't bad. Never mind. Here, blood-freezingly enough, were rules for operatives in the Canadian Ajax Skip-Tracer Agency! Here you go; this is it. She reads the rules; he seems to have crossed them out and rewritten them.

That was a good idea; she decides to add a few of her own:

9. Fill in the blanks as quickly as you can in the alloted time span; say seventy years.
10. Don't create beautiful suspects to chase on trains across Canada because they always evaporate at the end.
11. If this line of work doesn't suit you there's always unemployment insurance and retooling at the Ex-Skip-Tracer Rehabilitation Center in Spokane; they're doing great work with these people.
12. If you continue in this line of work you will be struck down by dread diseases and a special voodoo doll has been prepared for you and all who dare to follow the trail of MADAME ZONGA!

There. That ought to get the message across. The rules are always changing for whoever can rewrite them; following them is another matter.

STICKY WICKETS

"Why in hell would anybody want to know that?" she says. Men can always be distracted from asking personal questions by asking them questions about themselves. It gives her a sense of triumph and superiority. "You must have had a fascinating adolescence."

"No," he says. "I asked you."

They never really want to talk about you unless you've broken the law or have appeared from outer space.

"Where did you come up with seven different credit cards in three different names and which one is the real name?"

"What the hell is it your business? No, I don't want to go to breakfast. And no, I'm not getting off at the next station. My girl-friends lent me their cards. Because I'm going to Montreal to do some shopping. I'm going to buy myself a Mountie. I hear they have them on discount. And I really don't want you in my compartment this morning."

She hears him through the thin paneling as though they were in two different frames of a Spiderman comic.

But she doesn't have enough cash for breakfast and she doesn't want to use the charge card again in the dining room. Standing at the snack bar, looking tacky in high heels and the mink jacket, runs in her nylons, balancing a cup of coffee and a hot dog, potato chips— she finds she's afraid to try the Visa card even here. It's got to be him. He's a skip-tracer, a Mountie, a fed, a Visa or American Express detective of some kind, and he's going to say, okay, this is it; you're in it for fifty thousand dollars and what can she say? Just kidding? It's the story of her life. Wage slave, going zombie at the television station research files again, in for life plus a year. Just kidding. She spills the coffee all over the mink and suddenly begins crying. *I want to be helpless and taken-care-of. I want to be just as depressed and lonesome as I want to be. I don't want to be a New Woman, not right now. I'll be a New Woman tomorrow. I don't want to be smart or strong or brave. Not right now.*

"But you can't do that, ma'am," said the man at the snack bar, tapping her wrist. "We don't take Visa at the snack bar."

"Oh yes!" she says. "Yes, sorry," and she gives him back the hot dog.

The man at the snack bar stands there with the hot dog in his hand, angry, watching the lady in mahogany mink make a fast exit into the vestibule.

WHAT HE DOESN'T KNOW

"Where'd you get the ring?"

But if she acts like she doesn't know he knows, then he will all go away. It's hiding by putting your hands over your eyes; and then they laugh, and while they're laughing, you escape.

Life has required of her that she be on deck at all times, always on the periphery of her own story, with a full magazine. Your feelings never really count, not under those circumstances. Her exterior is expensive and shiny; it has cost her a lot of investment, time, and effort. It has done yeoman's service for years for both her and her employers. It is sturdy and canny; he doesn't know that, of course, and why should he?

"I didn't get it in the dining car, darling."

THE REAL STORY

They are moving through the urban corridor of warehousing and industrial parks. They are sitting in the club car drinking rum and Karma-Kola and suddenly, as if struck by an inspiration, he says,

"You're not really a railroad dick,"

and she says,

"Of course not,"

and he says,

"You're not really going to meet anybody in Montreal, are you?"

and she says,

"No,"

and he says,

"You grew up just where you said you did, in Oklahoma," and she doesn't remember if she told him Oklahoma or not but she says,

"Yes,"

and he says,

"You're changing trains in Toronto and going on down to the southern states on Amtrak,"

and she says,

"That's right,"

and he turns to her, taking hold of her wrist with a startling ferocity, and jerks her arm so hard the drink flies out of her hand, and he pulls her very close and says in his best low *Cockpit* voice,

"Listen you stupid little bitch, you're in it for $50,000 and everything seems just fine right now, but the problem is grand larceny, and if it's not me it'll be somebody else. You think it's a lark. You think all this is very high-rolling and exotic but in about thirty minutes you're going to wish like hell you'd kept on researching in that fucking Seattle television station or whatever it was you did there," and he gives her arm another jerk to get her attention because it appears she's faded off somewhere, into a world of bananas and guilt, and he says,

"You're going to take off to St. Louis and end up in some sleaze bar on the Landing eating imitation crab, thinking about who you'll call. You'll go through your address book and see who you know and you'll call them up and say, 'Come on down to Memphis with me. I got credit cards.' And you'll pick up some other sucker like me on the train,"
and she says,

"You know something, I've held down a job since I was seventeen years old and I got nothing to show for it but a train ticket to Memphis,"
and he says,

"And the other thing is, you're too old for anybody to teach you how to dress now,"
and she says,

"Come with me,"
and he says,

"I want to hit you. And you have crap spilled all over your blouse."

CUTTING OFF HER CREDIT

The suburbs of Toronto are going by, black and white, garroted by snow.

"I'm sorry," he says, "that you aren't really a railroad dick. You would have made a wonderful railroad dick."

"Oh, but I am one," she says. "I travel on trains, don't I? I ask questions, don't I?"

"Come on," he says. "I want to show you something."

He takes her by the arm and they go down into the lounge car and out into the vestibule. He takes her purse, opens it over her violent objections, removes the leather folder of credit cards, and starts pulling them out and whizzing them into the suburbs of Toronto. They fly sideways like little financial cleavers.

They stand looking at each other and with every mile they move toward either taking each other into custody or parting forever.

"Who the hell do you think you are?" she says, and doesn't wait for an answer. "Now I won't even be able to get a job!"

"Ah, darling, do not fall further into the ranks of crime," he advises her. "It pays too well."

Every dream is an adventure story, detective fiction, a mass paperback with You as the protagonist but not quite; the trick is, which one of you? And in every detective story there is the point where you finally see the person pursuing you, and everything is clear to both of you, and you have to run.

Run from your fate, run down the aisle of the sleeping cars and the dayniter, through the vestibules, shoving at the massive and resistant doors, run through the forward club car, run for the baggage car, don't wear high heels, don't wear little hats with veils, don't carry sharp objects you could fall on, don't carry heavy baggage by the handle, don't fumble with old stories, don't wait for men who say wait!, don't think about the past, don't get too involved. Don't be negative, just keep moving. The heroines of dreams and all their observations from moving cars.

THE ACTION SCENE

They're stalled in the Toronto train station, and he knows she's got to be breaking the sound barrier for the baggage car, and so he goes out the vestibule and down three steps like the Twentieth Century Limited. Hits the concrete and sees her, in that to-die dress and knock-em-dead mink coat, jump up on the baggage cart like a gazelle. The baggage man asks her what the hell she thinks she's doing and, from all the available evidence, she tells him in no uncertain terms. She has a pigskin bag in her hand and takes another leap down onto terra firma and is off like the space shuttle; no explosions. Why wait for the baggage claim to mangle your bags when you've got an escape to make? She's up the stairs like a kamikaze homing pigeon, and he's right after her. Double takes as perfectly innocent travelers coming down the escalator get bumped aside by a fleeing paperhanger, a skip-tracer in pursuit—only he just wants to tell her goodbye. He wants to tell her he's going to join her. He might say he'll share the story if only she'd stay in it. He wants to get out of the way of the point of view. He's going to say he'll write home and say *Wish you were here* on a tacky postcard of the CN tower. He'll say *Let's go live in a revolving restaurant.* It's raining cats, buckets and Albanians outside, and he decides to tell her she'll catch her death of narrative; and if she decides to hang around he'll find something they can do together—cook, sew, or fly DC-3s into Peru loaded with bales of cheap detective mysteries; they'll make a mint. They'll switch off being pilots and copilots. No kidding, wait; they run past advertisements for fur coats, rum, and underwear; he's gaining. She's running up the stairs—or if not running, then walking extremely fast—with one pigskin bag (leave the others, they're not important), and he's walking just as quickly beside her. She says:

"You wanted the story all to yourself after all, didn't you? Well, you can have it. You can have all the credit too, and the ideas; and being pursued by mysterious men isn't as fun as it used to be in the forties. Everything's changed. You can have it; there's enough either on this credit card or that credit card to get me to Memphis—I'll go to Memphis and disappear into exotic chaos. I knew it when you got on the train. I smelled a rat. You can have the entire story: the dialogue, the italicized sections, the uppercase titles, everything. You think you're very uppercase, don't you? I'm going to leave this hemisphere of print altogether. You will not meet me again, not on paper, anyhow. It's not so far from Memphis to Honduras. The page will jump out of your hand; it will be blown away on a long, angelic wind—a print hurricane of solid wind and hard copy—to a port city and disappearance: missing characters."

PARTING SCENE

He stops her at the curb outside the massive Toronto train station, in a heavy November rain. A scene of parting: is it necessary? Water falling off of things: water falling off her hat, and drops forming on the strands of the little veil (now ripped in places), and water forming and gathering on the mink shoulders, water dropping and running around the edges of her ears and off her earrings, and the toes of her high heels, water falling from his hands and wrists as he draws together the edges of the fox collar, and water on their lips as they kiss.

She seems to be fading out; or dying. Erased. He draws her close as people run past them toward the taxis at the curb and then he reaches into her pocket for the train ticket. He wants to make sure it says St. Louis or Memphis, or Waco; wherever it is she's going. And he's not sure she's there at all, anyway. He's occupying the center of the visual field so completely. He's sorry about this; confused. Is that her walking back into the gigantic station? Is that the noise of her thoughts; those trains? Is that the splashing of her footsteps and why did she leave? Why is he suddenly so hopelessly alone in the middle of the whole story? Our Hero. She is so wet she seems to have become counterfeit; or was it just him?

It was just him.

THE END: KING STREET

It has become his story without any effort on his part; it was preconstructed. He feels suddenly overwhelmed with loss, and so he tries to light a cigarette and takes on water. He feels he has lost something (a story) forever, that was of immense value, that would have made all the difference. He remembers what he thought he wanted was not what he really wanted, but who does? You know. He wanted the end of her story.

He stands in the rain in his hat like a book cover and hears the vague report of big ships unloading somewhere at a harbor. There is always a lake or river near these big cities in the east, and dense smoke, as if the city had taken a direct hit sometime in the night. Women avoid his glance as they walk by; they always do. He feels he's missed it, but he can have it yet, if he hurries, if he makes his mind up *now*, right now. *How can you leave,* he asks her, or thinks he did, *and walk off like that, and leave and go to Memphis?* Now he knows what it is he wanted, and the discovering is like standing on the shore of near space and looking out beyond to the Horsehead Nebula, thinking, *If only I let go I'll float off into the hot and glowing*

*rainbow of the interior, the Bengalese crown jewels; and if only you would
not get on the train south, and if only I could relocate you, and if only the
noises of the ships' horns didn't keep sounding a narrative about something
I almost had, and that I missed;* and he walks quickly into the train
station.

THE BEGINNING

She's been waiting for two hours and if he doesn't show up within
another fifteen minutes, she's going on without him. The entire cargo
of vintage *Black Mask* magazines, a complete set starting in 1920, was
securely crated and waiting at the Frobisher Bay field. She put down
the book she had been reading, a bit of fluff called *A Manual of
Etiquette for Ladies Crossing Canada by Train*. She's waiting in a snack
joint just west of the big high school gymnasium; a geodesic dome
made to look like an igloo. Clever, these Canadians. . . . Can you
imagine, looking just like an igloo! Wow. The local inhabitants must
have been snowed. The snack joint was owned by an Italian who also
ran a couple of taxis—Happy Bob's Polar Cab Company. Summertime
in Frobisher Bay meant pack ice grinding down on several beached
freighters out in the bay, and bad weather. If he didn't get here in
fifteen minutes she'd go without him.

"Waiting for somebody?"

"What were you doing, counting your brain cells?"

"Forget the snappy repartee; the guy's going to take off without
us if we don't get loaded and go."

"Is this Dane really going to pop for the whole set? Is this all
they have to read in Greenland?"

"He's an international dealer holed up in Nuuk."

"That sounds like you made it up."

"Smuggling rare books isn't as commonplace as it used to be."

Snappy repartee continues as they race in Happy Polar Bob's taxi
for the airport. She and he kiss madly; he runs his hands through her
short blond hair. Air Greenland's twin otter spins its propellers. She
tosses the book out the window; there'll be magazines on the plane—
Cockpit, maybe.

In this country you must think carefully
about what all human beings
have in common.
    All human beings like things grouped
in bunches, they wear something around
    their waists, they break all the
commandments and are sorry or not sorry.

Human thought, untrained,
is a series of broken details.
    Everyone's history begins
with a victory over time and space
and the terrible earth
foundation legends, gold rushes,
a battle which we won and
    where something was irretrievably lost.

    In my windows the hanging lamp reflects
like a moon, a fresh yellow pie.
    The real moon is masked by spruce,
the ravens and dogs
search for sleeping places.
    A great stream of people found and
lodged themselves here, ran into another
group of people and derailed.
    Bound on the iron lakes, in the rain
of paper directives and policies,
    we have forgotten what we knew
about each other,
    we do not even have the same legends
about the moon, or one does
and the other forgot.
    We have to remind ourselves
about the moon's ice and the dry, early wind

the snow burnt off,
things grouped in bunches, the commandments,
the broken details. About our compromise with time
and space and the terrible earth.

Blank on the black cove
black rocks and the sea like a meadow, extending,
extending.
I am a caretaker.
I am alone, and only concerned with the dirty seashells
and crabshells
and lost hats tipping themselves in the undertow.
They have lost the heads they used to contain and now
they wave out of sight.

The tide sinks back. All this stone at close range!
Not like my friends,
or as they were, full of purposes and awards and the
day after tomorrow.
The sea is too bright; and at the end of this island,
a lamp I cannot light,
the long walk home.

The Atlantic is a family of savages, all of them different;
the currents, the coves,
mainstreams and undertows and the long, blank
sky between me and disaster.
This is the world, then.
No one will ever believe me.

The sun rises behind the power station over the Ungava hills, it comes up in a neon fog, minute crystals swarm in its shafts like anti-insects. Behind me the land rises and rises as if it were making the same statement over and over only louder each time. A river of glass freezes down from these mountains in aquamarine and jade. Before a gale the clouds are hard and white and without shadows like milk poured into clear water. When they strike the mountains I expect them to make a noise. They do make a noise; at night I can hear them, hard and grinding. Henri and I walk through the village to find that lights are spearing upward like announcements or signals for help.

At night the power station sends out its green-white carbide light and in gales when snow streaks past in horizontal shouts the light fades and recovers and fades again. Our lamps fade and recover and fade again. With every equinoctial storm that tears through here we both lose and gain. The light of the power station is an emerald, like the ones in the foreheads of idols on the late show. I wear it on top of my mind. I fade and recover, my electricity walking in the waves of gales. My imagination becomes an arctic, laced with jade rivers. I feel like a land above some treeline, infinitely detailed, stripped by gale-force winds of anything that gets in the way. I have everything I need except the sun and it comes without warning. I seem to be growing through latitudes, and in gales my single carbide light remains and holds. Whatever I now possess is true and whatever I do not have is too bad; including the announcements, including the signals for help.

We got to where we were television programs.
We ran on.
There were adventures in the Amazon,
in city streets, in the thirties,
our parents watched us, relentlessly.
We lived in a Japanese chassis
and birds sat on our aerials.
"What did you do today?" they asked,
and we began entertaining them,
relentlessly.
I cried when I won a Hollywood Square
with a weekend in Kapuskasing.
It was all wrong
and they turned us off
to sit blank and gray until
we could learn to do it right.
Then they went to bed and had
reluctant primal scenes.
We prepared news for the next morning's show;
fires, weather reports,
kidnappings.

Sometimes people come on in one big
unmuffled roar of engines and your
window won't keep anything out.
A city in perpetual torment,
the lives of those who have been discarded
are swept up by the garbagemen.
They come by like undertakers;
their quick forensic jobs have supplied me
with a thousand thoughts but no
metaphors;
they come to the conclusions
we have thrown away.

Long ago (this is a story)
an exploding star became a lighthouse
somewhere to the left of the equator.

Solar winds blew its hair around.
After such a birth,
what kind of life awaits it?

My mast draws circles
around the lighthouse–star
waves like hair comb themselves,

we are running northwestward
down an unknown coast.
O nocturnal ballads,
ship of the auroral ocean,

we are marked with moon spots.
I feel the rush of water
lay on the rudder like a giant snake,

the tiller shakes,
the water talks to me in this morse.
Left and right
the red and green running lights

shine through glass walls of fresh water.
Sailing is one of the varieties of love,
it is one of the varieties of solitude,

it is prayer-dancing with the new world.

Language has flown away from me
in one of the varieties of devotion to water.

To devotion,
to lighthouses.

I live on the prow of the *Griffon*
dressed in copper bands,
a woman of salt and cedar.

I am pure decoration,
like a hood ornament.

Life here on the *Griffon*'s nose is variable.
I was carved by a master carver
in Montreal,
a sort of chiseling obstetrician.
He gave me form,
it was his thick hands I sprang from,
shedding chips and shavings.
Men instinctively like me
and no wonder.

At night the men speak to me.
I animate,
under their voices everything works right,
I am intelligent and funny,
I have that fine, smooth skin of women
who never move their faces.

By day the landscape goes by.
There are birds, rock, other things.
The wind gives us motion or not.

Now that the ship is broken
and foundered on Russel Island,
the men have deserted me to live among
        the Indians
if they are lucky
(those women, quick with paddles,

dressed in vermilion and minks).
I float face-up in this
primeval freshwater bath.

Being alone is a terrible surprise.
It's like landing on the moon.

Look at the world.
There are waxwings overhead
and a shoreful of trees,
pebbles like eggs in the peacock-colored water.
I float among their bread and their boots.

What was it they wanted?
Did they know what they really wanted?
There is one more question
in this series of questions
which is
what do I want
which I never ask,
being wooden, being a decoy,

for the next crew,
the next ship,

for whoever will settle
on this perilous water, which is
perfectly clear.

They sail quickly, nervously along the limestone shores. They imagine the cracked rock below them to be the remains of cities (what else). They hope to find the aborigines so they can be admired or hated, either one. They are sailing neck and neck with the new world.

Each night as their ship lays its insecure anchor, dragging gripless over the smooth paving stones of the bottom, the men wrestle in dreams. The ship's boy dreams someone has stolen his new shoes. The bosun dreams that a pistol has gone off in his hand. The cook dreams that his arms have turned into anchors and the captain dreams he is moving a piano.

(Occasionally in their dreams there are people who come riding up from the direction of Altair, they are glassed-in, like church windows, they are all color and illumination. And the ones who come from southwest of Antares are full of words, they have the words.)

On some days small joys creak out, they escape, fly loose like young gulls still spotty in their juvenile feathers. The men say "Look, a headland, around this one will be the passage to China." On a thin point which seems to float a few inches above the water at a mile's distance are the people who live around here, waiting for them to do something besides sail in different directions and argue with themselves. The aborigines wave things, they have built a smoky fire of green ash. Now the men remember. They are here, on the Georgian Bay, it was where they were sailing after all. They had been thinking of Cathay, potentates, silk, and minor grudges. They may have traded with the aborigines, they might have given them mirrors so they could look at themselves instead of out at the world. The men would have become anxious, talking quickly, trading words like reassurances, any words.

The aborigines would have become anxious as well, and therefore silent. This would have made the Bretons even more nervous, this silence. They would have talked faster, sweated adrenaline (you can smell it), turned to see what the captain was going to do or think, the captain would have wondered what the aborigines were going to do or think. Each human shape either threatens or promises, we cannot stop to observe who they are, what they look like, if they have souls or no souls. Quick, move, either they have terrible needs or we do, one or the other, and one or the other will get what they want.

White pine seep their resinous odor and gulls with red dots on their beaks leap up and scream. The ship's boy realizes there is going to be trouble. The sailors in their aboriginal fear suddenly imagine things, a thick-handled fish knife flies out of somebody's hand from somewhere. What in god's name can we be thinking of, and here we are alone on these shores, this is the Georgian Bay, beyond us yet another freshwater ocean and what have we been dreaming of all this time? We have not looked at the world for so many years. Here it is. Shafts of sunlight stalk the water like the stilts of immense cranes. The waves are like foil, on their surface moves the crushed velvet of the wind. They say Christ released us from the terrors of this un- known continent but they do not mean it. Maybe they want to be released from each other or themselves but there are no prayers for this and god doesn't work that way.

In the northeast a storm, indigo blue and shot with ball light- ning, is under construction. The big ones come from the east, this harbor is not safe. This one will drive the rivets from their seating and the ship onto the stony shore. The ship's boy and all of them turn to the suddenly building wind. The cook's cheese papers fly loose like telegrams.

I'll run away now and hide out, says the ship's boy, while they fight each other. In his mind he goes feral like the wolf-child of Auvergnon. This is a red pine, this is a spruce. These are my feet. What was I thinking of, serving the captain and winding line, here I am in possession of numberless stars, crossing both time and spaces of thin water. Day by day he plans on curing himself of people, there must be a medicine that will work into other philosophies. He dreams of cinnamon factories and people in the glassy forest who lie down each night with friendly griffons. The shelves of the new world are empty of bosuns and cooks. If I stay away from them I can't be caught.

(The cities are already here. The streets are here, laid out and packaged, the mind gropes toward packages, barracks, mines. They have already brought diseases and imported food. We do not even know what our hands are doing, much less our feet, as we walk through these tangled mental systems, but we seem to be moving in a vaguely westerly direction. We are nothing if not neat. We dream of rocky, lighted shores.)

Running through stands of cedar, he hears the captain and sailors shouting. Small darters wing and crackle in the grass. Ahead in his flight is the legend of the boy chased by a rolling head, a logic of tangible qualities. On both sides the beige, flaming foxtail grasses of the new world race with him, neck and neck. Somewhere ahead he will have to pay the ferryman, it will be the Loon, dressed in frost and oils, what the price will be he doesn't know, he will only want to cross the water, this water here. The cedar lifts its lacy hands as if to applaud, but hesitates, shocked by winds.

People said the captain was killed in the surf
because we ran out of red cloth,
but it was different.

His arm went up and the rest of him went under,
he was all white and flash.
The clothes came floating back first,
the rags we knew so well, a shoe.
The wind jumped up out of the headlands
and all the sails filled over the wreck
with a great noise, like you hear from a crowd
when something happens,
an explosion of white sail
and the wind was blowing the wreck toward anything,
toward whatever was ahead.

He was cutting bacon for their captain
and he sliced off his fingertip and it bled.
The people stared, it was the final clue,
the end of the mystery novel.
Later when he waded ashore again
and demanded men to help repair the ship,
somebody killed him.

He should have told them in the first place,
it's too late now,
we want to prove we are people,
we have failures and hopes and women.
We still seem dangerous
but now we are killable.

And now we are here forever.
The snow will come in columns.

We can try to say we were just passing through.
As a last, desperate gamble,
we will try to act like human beings.

A poem like this is an adventure
in a minute boat. The stones on the shore
people pick up for playing *wari*
    seem like glacial erratics.
It is like sailing on a poplar leaf,
    only the stars keep their same size.

There are reasons for this world.
Nobody has trouble with men here,
or landladies. We do not live on paychecks.
A planet-sized drop of dew rolls from a
spruce needle, it is the size of a supernova,
its surface gravity trembles
and breaks, the collapsing shells
of atoms.

I would make this poem
even smaller
if I
cd

Our parents were hungry;
in the smoke of old campfires,
in the middle of a retreat
	they fed from us as if we were Easter
wafers,
	granting nutrition
and soul food at once.

	Around ourselves
we set up barbed wire fences.
	We were not churches after all.
	What gleams came through us, we
wondered, like stained glass?

I am on the prow of a great ship called the *Kristan*
wallowing out the East Pass. We are lit up like a city.
At night, when the mist like tear-gas drives your eye
inward,

we are mistaken for Buffalo or Port Credit. I wave goodbye
tearfully to my friends, my hair drawn out in a bush of adieux.
We roll and slew with a great load in the holds, talking about
being gone.

Day after day the green, polluted flood drains toward Gaspé.
That's my water-supply. It carries with it flotsam, cargoes
of diesel-oil and gasoline rainbows in which a soaked, hopeful figure
occasionally drowns.

Memory begins with the feet, spreading
like a narcotic or frostbite headward.
The Lake, like a rainspout, is naked and close, a million shades
of metal.
Everywhere the sky is lit up with cities.

A tangle of black calligraphy,
taut as a telephone cord during an important call.

He has the arrogance of Texas oil.
His eyes dart little migraines.

His trickling, scaly currents erect on their own coils.

Slimmer and thinner his forepart curves
like a question mark to the hypnotized water—

the clear, brown lens of these hills
and oaks. A high-power line dips in the pool

                                          sip

sip

drops like rhinestones splintering
unwinding like a black umbilicus
his slick glitter is perfectly voiceless and thin.

Everything the loon sings about is
monumental and jeweled.
Everything matters
and floats.
They take nothing calmly.
These must be domestic arguments
out there in the bay, other women,
divorces.

We are held by two anchors,
bow and stern,
the sails in their crisp bags crackle.
Later I will have dreams
of being rammed in the forepeak
as we sink in columns of
fairy bubbles toward whatever
the bottom holds.

Pines full of turpentine bend
with bitter grace over the shore.
They are right.
Everything matters.

We used to have wives.
They carried and did things around the house;
what, I don't know.
Rugs cleaned themselves,
my suitcoats and this blue middy
walked to the cleaners,
the sheets put themselves to bed.

She was too young to marry
and I was too young to know what I wanted.
Immature at twenty,
suddenly there were these babies
who saw us as adults.

We became fixed, somehow,
as tomcats are fixed,
what you call neutered,
stopped,
as in a photographer's solution.
I took a job on a cigarette package
and she became a sort of turtle,
wearing her house on her back.
In this life of amber
we outwaited the children,
fixed in amber
like ancient hornets.

Now we are released.
Our children release us into these new fashions.
Sails draw up. I am sailing away like Jack.
The boat bails itself,
I do my own washing. I have left that house
for a life

where I do my own dishes.
She thought I needed her for that,
she would have staked her life on it.

This is the bus that goes to Montreal. Ha ha! it says,
edging nervously along the highway, full of passengers
and savoir-faire. Someday it will not go anywhere but
straight up, taking us all with it. This bus may be
dutiful, even glamorous, but it has a mind of its own.
It slides to a halt in Dorval and self-destructs.
William, William, I am not laughing anymore, get me off
    this bus!

This is the bus that used to go to Buffalo. Now the
sad springs have rebounded and its crippled emotions
weep, weep oil. Oil is the sorrow of the Buffalo bus.

The highway is a study in ballistics, full of Pontiacs
and captured citizens. Trucks lay out volumes of monoxide,
their blunt fronts are a ride to nowhere. The Kenora bus
is as shy as a pike. It is a big shoe in which live
the feet of the Anishnabek.

From Vancouver comes a double-decker bus, nearly finished.
I have told so many lies about the Vancouver bus, it is a
horror-show, seeing it all come true. What memories of
opium and green piles of sulphur! I am bracketed between
declarations of love and disgust for the Vancouver bus.

The Winnipeg bus will abandon you on the highway and go on.
Out there is a bald place where you will be left without
hope or pity or mercy for the infirm. A Chinese girl
ran off to Regina on this bus. None of that is any
    of my business.

I wish my ticket said somewhere. It is a ticket of fate I got
out of a fat machine. It says I am a hillbilly, and my people
are lost, and the bus doesn't go there anymore.

There is little time to write between rearranging everything so that Mama can reach whatever she needs when I'm gone, and the television going on and Bonnie and Nettie coming in, and me going over to Bonnie and Nettie's, and running around to look at graveyards. This is why I'm sending you The Map, so you can get the vital signs of this universe oriented.

Nettie and I were over at Salt Fork graveyard looking for distant cousins of mine among the gravestones; Nettie's little boy is buried over there. Mama said, "But, honey, Salt Fork is way over there, those aren't Our People."

Salt Fork is *seven miles away.* You'd think it was Tennessee or something. However, even though Salt Fork is in the remote relational distance, they are at least Known To Our People or Married Into Our People; Salt Fork has the Youngers and the Findlays and the Crocketts and the Beckers.

When my mother was feeling better last week, she and I and Aunt Mayme drove over to the old New Lebanon graveyard and found my great-great-great-grandfather Chesley Burnett; he's surrounded by three wives, Sarah and Elizabeth and Mary, and I am sure they are washing his socks in heaven. I heard stories from a very old lady about those Cumberland Presbyterian communities down there. She said at Wednesday night prayer-meetings they sent the kids upstairs to sleep so the grown-ups could pray in peace, and my great-great-uncle Denver Huffman used to chuck his shoes down the stairwell at the grown-ups and then get sent to the barn for it. These are the kinds of things that are passed down as episodes in the family epics: chucking shoes down stairwells.

I am keeping myself busy by tracing the family, my mother's family. They were here early but poor, but respectable, but *early.* Burnetts filed for land in 1819. Maybe they grew here. Maybe God made them out of combustible Presbyterian and Baptist flammables. Maybe they went through the gill stages of evolution right here in the muddy flooding LaMine and Blackwater rivers, maybe they chucked themselves up on the banks and were stricken with the Revealed Word and filed for land as soon as they grew fingers and a forebrain. My father's people are all from down in the Ozarks in southeast Missouri and never came from anywhere else except Tennessee. They went through the Paleolithic there and then emerged into agriculture and the Early Neolithic in Butler County. And then in the thirties they took agriculture a step further and ran moonshine across the Mississippi into Little Egypt by the tank load. That was my uncle Tucker—but let that go for now. I told you I'd write you all about the Blackwater people.

I went to church again last Sunday, to Peninsula Church, where all Our People are buried, the last four generations, anyway. And when I came into church, an old lady came up to me and said, "Hi there, honey, do you remember me? I'm Daisy Castle and the last time I saw you, you were seven years old and running out of Lola Mae Self's house. She was chasing you with a peach switch, and you were yelling, 'But I ain't treated this way at home!'"

My God, I was lying even then. Lola Mae and Jimmy Self and all the Self cousins were the ones that used to eat fried squirrel heads. They'd have squirrel for supper and they'd sit around and argue over who got to eat the head. Can you believe that? I loved them. And I can only barely remember Lola Mae chasing me out of the house with a peach switch. It must have been the old Potter house. I don't know where they all are now. They moved away, and Jimmy died, and then Lola Mae got married to a man who had been mowed by a hay-mower and they lived on the insurance money, and the oldest daughter, Maggie Lee, married into the Air Force and lives in South Carolina and has a beauty shop. Junior drives a truck and Raymond is a deputy sheriff in Audrain County. I remember driving around with Raymond when he was old enough to drive. He was a big cousin, who would always take the little ones in the back. The best place was Mash-It Hill, which you will see marked on The Map. This is a place where, if you stand on the accelerator, coming around the bend and head off over the brow of the hill at top speed you'll leave the ground with all four wheels and briefly have the zero-gravity experience. The Right Stuff. Whenever I'm driving back from Loller's Station with my nephews, they yell, "Stand on it, Aunt Polly! Mash it!" But I've never had the courage to go over it at more than 75 mph. *It is said* Bonnie Rapp went over it at 100 mph with no ill effects.

The soybean problem continues. As I mentioned in my last letter, the soybean silos down by the river took on water in the flood and the soybeans swelled up and busted and there are rotting heaps of them all along the railroad tracks. They are decaying in the roads and leaking into the town well. The more they move them around with earthmovers and trucks, the more they stink, and today it's alarming. Birds are laying close to the ground and horses are staggering in the fields. When they start in on a heap of them with the blade, steam starts rolling up from the fermentation and people walk around town with their scarves over their faces.

I went into Jack's, the general store, to look for somebody to help me jump-start Mama's car and ran into Bo and Jerry Nowlan and Simple Billy Sligo. Simple Billy is my fifth cousin. He's about thirty-five and retarded and merry and good. His brother Pete Sligo used to make him sleep in the attic without any heat and Simple Billy would sleep curled around the chimney flue to stay warm until Nettie and Jerry Nowlan decided he could get some kind of assistance, and got it for him by filling out all the right papers, and now Simple Billy has his own trailer and is warm if a bit ragged. I am sending a picture of him and Jerry Nowlan when they came to jump-start the car. Billy gets his check every month and Jerry gives him some of it, with which he buys enough soda and snuff to last him the while, and Jerry keeps aside the rest to give him a little at a time. Pete Sligo goes down to the town office and tells Bonnie Rapp that he's a secret agent for the FBI and that all these people are after him. Bonnie Rapp listens to all this stuff when she's making out the water bills. She's town clerk. She had this elderly fellow come in to talk to her one time; he usually only gets out for funerals. In trying desperately to make conversation, he said, "You know, I never knew your mama when she was alive but she made the prettiest corpse I ever saw."

Bo asked me to sit and have coffee with him. I've known Bo for several lifetimes and only recently found out his entire name is George Hibbard Bodine. Three years ago when I was down here visiting I was walking Mom's dog out by the Old Marshall Place, on the back road to Salt Fork, this great shark-colored pickup with a gunrack came up beside me and Bo stuck his head out and said, "You're Polly! I know you! You know me too, but you probably forgot! My name's Bo!" And I said, "I know you!" And he said, "You know what? Every

goddamn son of a bitch in this county has voted Republican but me!"
And he mashed it, and went away from there.

Last summer I was walking the road out to Wildcliff and he drove
up in a different-colored pickup and said, "You like Russell Stover,
honey? Here, pick one." And shoved this big box of Russell Stover
chocolates out the window at me, so I picked one, and said good day
and he stood on the accelerator and departed. You know how Bo makes
a living? When he was in the army thirty-five years ago, something
fell on his head—a general, probably, or something with a lot of
brass—and he had to have a head operation and he's been living well
on a full U.S. Army disability pension ever since. (Now as I am
reading the galleys, I realize that I have misled you in this matter.
Bo gave me a ride over to Howard County this morning, across the
Missouri River, to go buy a salt-cured ham, and he said he got his
head wound from shrapnel in 1944. He drove his tank over a landmine
in Krefeld, Germany. He was at D-day too. When he takes his hat
off it looks like the Missouri Pacific ran over his head. And then he
changed the subject to how he takes his bird dog, Lulu, to Big John's
every morning and buys her biscuits and gravy for breakfast. Bo used
to have whiskey for breakfast, but he gave that up. He is an expert
at revealing one story inside another story inside another story. It
requires not only skill and experience but an immense amount of
material.) There is absolutely nothing wrong with Bo's head at all.
He buys a new pickup every year and doesn't have much to do except
vote Democrat and hang around Jack's. He is a Good Old Boy. He
Hangs Around. Five years ago he took my brother-in-law Roger out
to drink and play cards and Roger took twenty bucks off the Younger
boy, Dale Younger—of the Youngers—and they probably thought he
was a St. Louis cardsharp so they decided to sit out in the pickup and
drink. You can sit out on Old Old Forty and drink in a pickup. There's
Interstate Seventy, which is a maelstrom of transports and cars, and
then there's Old Forty, which it superseded, and then there's Old
Old Forty, which was the oldest highway of all, with long stretches
of still-extant concrete on which people can sit in their pickups and
drink without much chance of getting hit by a passing car.

I sat down with Bo in Jack's store and had coffee. I said, "Bo,
are we cousins?" and he said, "No, darlin', but we had the same

great-aunt Leona. I'm related on her side and you're related on Uncle John's side." So I said, "Then your mother is a Mercer." And he said, "That's right." And I said, "Great-Aunt Leona had some strict ideas." And he said, "All them Mercers had strict ideas, honey. They were all stubborn. Every damn one of them Mercers were stubborn. And let me tell you whut, Aunt Leona was the *humblest*."

Aunt Leona belonged to a fundamentalist sect that people around here call the Blackstockings because all the women wore black stockings and long dresses. Every Thing Wasn't Allowed. When my cousin Patty and I used to go stay with them, we would roll up our jeans legs under our dirndl skirts and walk innocently down the road and, upon clearing the farmhouse around the edge of Rattlesnake Hill, we would hang up our skirts on a fence and then go ride Hemp Williams's horses. They were Abner and Sweetpea. The skirts were those vast gathered print ones of 1957. They were like flags! One time Abner and Sweetpea got away from us and went rocketing uncontrollably into Uncle John and Aunt Leona's front drive and there we were, riding in shorts!! But Aunt Leona never chided us, no. She was just sorry you were going to Hell. She regretted it enormously and would only gaze at you with great sorrowful eyes and left out religious tracts for you to find, and if, in the immense boredom of the evenings when the Seth Thomas was crashing away like some kind of upright Marching Band of Time, and the hogs and cows and dogs snorted and snored in the barn under the hill, and constellations slid sideways past Chimney Rock and I sat there and wondered what would I do when I got big, and how you made money to buy cars, because I wanted a car, and I wanted to Sin and Drink Beer. (Where do you get beer? How do you get cars? How do you make money? Do men have to get everything for you or can you get it yourself? If you write, do you have to write like Mark Twain, or do you have to write like Nancy Drew?) Because, after all, I was big, or getting there; and Uncle John stared in a strange drifty way at the wall and rocked with squeaks back and forth; sometimes he said Well, Duck . . . as if he were about to say something more; he called Aunt Leona "Duck," and the whole place was right out of the 1840s, when people were of course Holier, and Campbellites Walked the Earth, and if, by chance, you happened to pick up one of these religious tracts which promised Hellfire and

Crispy Sinners if you were Unrighteous, and a front-row seat in the Heavenly Choir if you joined up, she would look at you with a pleased smile and say, "Well, at *least* you're *reading* it."

She had you. What could I say—no, I wasn't reading it? I was eating it? I was checking it for pecker tracks? With this kind of upbringing, all her children led Interesting Lives. Lola Mae married Jimmy Self and took after people with peach switches. And the sons, Walter and Wilbur, used to do Practical Jokes. One of their practical jokes was to "take somebody for a pickup ride." They'd get somebody in the seat between them so the victim couldn't bolt out of the truck, and drive at top speed down the country roads with one wheel in the ditch and the other on the blacktop smashing down every sign they came upon; YIELD signs and STOP signs and 20 MPH signs and DEER CROSSING signs. You only went in a pickup with those guys once. They put hog manure in the hired man's sandwiches and burnt down the storage shed where all my grandpa and grandma's possessions were, the time Grandpa went to Kansas to look for work in the Depression. Wilbur joined the army and finally gave up the Practical Jokes, except on a minor scale, but Walter never stopped. It got into Assault and Arson. One time he came back from California with his wife and daughters "until things cooled off out there." He'd got into an argument with his employer and had thrown gasoline around the work site where he was carpentering, and set the place on fire. At that time Aunt Leona had finally decided that electricity wasn't sinful, so he occupied himself with helping wire the farmhouse. He laid hold of a high-voltage live wire and fried himself. *Ha ha, Walter,* said God. *How do you like my little Practical Joke?* And let me tell you whut, Aunt Leona was the *humblest.*

I am right now over at Aunt Mayme's workshop, where she used to have her beauty shop. It's very quiet and it looks out over the Crittendens' house. They were Good Family and Now Look. There's a blue-tick hound with a broken leg, lying under their porch, whining. It's the most dreadful sound. But they won't take him to the vet. If he survives, they'll be happy and not out any money, of which they don't have any. Jack has cut them off credit. This is Trigg Avenue here, a dirt road going on out into the country. Down from here two blocks is where the *black section* used to be. Yes, indeed, in a town of *two hundred fifty* people. There are both black and white families living there now. That's where Mrs. Poindexter and her daughter Vera Lee live. They got flooded out in the flood and they had a time moving Mrs. Poindexter. At ninety-two, she's the oldest resident of Blackwater and she's blind and has become silently impatient with the world of the living. They're back in their house now, but they were moved to three different places during the flood.

That's where I saw the man with the double-bitted ax taking apart a mobile home; he was standing on top of it, absolutely destroying it, like some Luddite rising out of the cold lonely grave to smite unto fragments this piece of shoddy shit. Pieces of bathroom paneling with fish printed on it were flying, and the front had already come down, so you could see right there what mobile homes were made out of if you had ever wondered what mobile homes were made out of. His house next to it was an old frame building which seems to sit there and *emit* trash; junk; bits and remnants of anything that could go on a car or in a house; sections of stoves and electric fans, plastic ducks, dogs, tires, clay pots, kindling, tin dishes, advertising from a gas station that said REGULAR and HI-TEST. He said, "Come on up here and give me a hand, why don't you?" and I said, "I guess I was born lazy," and he said, "I tey you whut, I don't have the money to have her moved off, so I thought, well, I'll just take her apart where she stands. I had another one here before, but it got to where it wasn't any good either, so I had that one hauled off, and I got this here one for the kids, but there ain't nobody but me here now, and the town'll make you pay taxes on it, so I thought I'd just take her apart where she stands. There's a fellow over there's going to use this here tin for the cow shed and another fellow going to buy the plywood off me and put it up for his pigs to get under, and so I'm just busting her up right here. What's this dog you got here?" and I said, "This here's my mother's dog," and he said, "You know something? Me and some guys went out wolf-hunting and we sat there all damn night, about fifteen men and an ungodly amount of dogs, and they wasn't a wolf to be seen. I tey you whut, can't dance and it's too wet to plow. Well, if I don't see you before, you have a good Christmas."

I didn't grow up here full-time; my dad moved around from town to town in Cooper and Pettis counties and then down in the Ozarks. I was born in the Ozarks and then we came back here because my mother is From Here. This is the center of the Known Universe. And with my grandfather, it was the same thing; down to the Ozarks and then back to the Missouri River counties. I used to think myself unfortunate because I went to five different grade schools and two high schools. But my mother and her two sisters were talking the other night, and it appears Maxie Belle went to nineteen different schools, and Mom and Mayme to something like that. My grandad just never stopped moving. He barbered and he ran dance halls, and he was a constable and a coroner and sometimes he farmed. I just remember him barbering and farming, but the three sisters remember the dance halls and the rest of it; they remember when Old Bagnell burnt down and when the dam was finished and the water began to back up over Lynn Creek and flooded the town site and the Army Corps of Engineers dynamited the town. This was all during the Depression. They moved everywhere and lost things and had dogs and monkeys and Grandpa could play any kind of a musical instrument.

Maxie Belle remembers moving out of Lynn Creek in the Ozarks in an old Hudson, I think, pulling an overloaded trailer full of all their household possessions, with most of the town waving goodbye, when the trailer hit a bump and tipped over, spilling everything onto the blacktop. So half the town came out and helped them put everything back into the trailer and then they camped out in people's farmyards. "We were just like a bunch of gypsies and mother used to cry, she was so humiliated." So my mother married young, and they went to St. Louis to work in the war industries before Dad went into the Navy and they took me and Kenneth. And Maxie Belle left home and came to live with them, and they bought pretty clothes and looked beautiful. They were all beautiful. Aunt Mayme was Responsibly Beautiful, and the oldest, and Maxie Belle was Dark and Wild and Beautiful, and she was the youngest, and Mom was Ethereally Beautiful, and she was in the middle. War work!! That was a phrase of power and magic and cash to that generation—right out of the Ozarks and all of a sudden women could get jobs, they could buy clothes! Maxie Belle and my dad's sisters all worked at the C-ration factory in St. Louis breaking eggs and throwing them at each other, so they got fired, and then they went to work in the Old Vienna Potato Chip Factory, and Maxie Belle jumped into the potato chips for a lark, and so they got fired from that job. They used to take me on the streetcar in their beautiful new clothes and tell people I was an orphan and that they were taking me to the Foundling's Home, they'd found me in a basket.

They found me at the tiny old French house on Tenth and Lafayette near Soulard Market, is where they found me, and I envision my mother looking out the long windows past the courtyard, wondering when they were going to bring me home out of the huge city streets with taxis and sailors and dangerous white slavers. And what my grandmother saved out of the wreck of all their moving around was quilts. They are cheaply made and easily transported and she did them beautifully. Aunt Mayme got out Grandma's Wedding Ring Quilt, and we spread it out on the floor and looked for our dresses and shirts and things in it. Aunt Mayme found a red-and-white polka dot that she'd worn when she was pregnant with Glen, and Mama found a blue check from a blouse of hers. These were all feedsack prints from the Salem flour mill and they all said it must have been made in the forties, but then I found two of mine; one was a green print with yellow and red pencils on it and I remember it from third or fourth grade, and I remember sitting in the schoolroom at Alexander School, so it had to be in the early fifties. I remember so horribly being lost and terrified at that school, and furious with everything, and my hair was cut off in ugly bangs. I was tired of my father's rages and his breaking dishes, and I was reading far ahead of my class and I wanted to go away and live in another time warp.

And I found another patch of mine, a lavender. I recall struggling into that playsuit to go milk with Grandad at 6:30 a.m. on the farm down in Dent County. I always got to go with him, not Kenneth or Sunny, just me! I didn't know anything about the tipped-over trailer or the dance halls or my grandma being humiliated. (She came from Good Family and Now Look.) He was so kind and so whiteheaded. With his wonderful harmonica, he knew miles of courthouse ballads, and I got to go with him every morning. He was the Emperor of Dent County with his tiny barn and a brass bedstead for a farmyard gate. The shafts of light hit his catalpa tree at an odd, delightful angle, and it would come in in bars between the barnboards, and the swallows and martins would appear in them as if they had been teleported there—and at that hour, the train would come down from Cherry Knoll, a miniature steam engine the size of a Russell Stover candy box, with flossy steam trailing after it and drifting over the ragged tacky fields of Queen Anne's lace and the sassafras trees and the oak, the pond steamed and the whole Ozarks remade itself after the looseness of night and the demented whippoorwills. It remade itself leaf by leaf, and the cows were full of cream and wild onions. My grandfather had just commandeered the entire world.

Grandma put the whole quilt together, linking everybody's stories. I bet there's a piece of one of Aunt Leona's Blackstocking dresses in there and shirts of Wilbur and Walter's, and one of Maxie Belle's snazzy war-work dresses, and my brother's brown-stripe shirt, Sunny's yellow dotted swiss, and who knows? Maybe something from Bo and Simple Billy or even a Younger, and behind those patches are all their stories they remember when they were wearing them, and all those stories are sewn into this white-trash patchwork lifetime theater; just the simplest remnants, which can evoke the most overwhelming memories, caught up in the starkest kind of elemental plot. There are hundreds of stories of people stitched up in all the big circles of this Wedding Ring Quilt.

I wish we still made them.

I am just thinking of my grandmother, Lula Belle King Racy, with her immense history of Cumberland Presbyterians coming from Virginia out of the Shenandoah and through the Cumberland Gap, the men all on fire with the Revealed Word and the women pregnant and stitching up these mnemonic devices, everybody's tiny stories, and that Grandma had chosen to include those two pieces of mine stuns me. And all gratitude has in it the elements of surprise and recognition.

I keep finding bits of my character; yesterday I was reading, with utter horror, letters I had written to my parents which are tucked away in the old-photographs box. I seem to have put an enormous amount of effort into being Falsely Known, as Vicki Hearne puts it; I was full of Important Careers, with Exciting Boyfriends, at one time I posed as a Coed and another as a Young Girl Reporter. In contrast, I ran into one of my father's letters from the South Pacific during the war, from on board a destroyer escort, the *Finnegan*:

My darling wife, In each letter I send to you I try to always say in some way that I love you dearly, but just saying it, darling, seems to do so very little. I want to be home so much, for you and the children are constantly on my mind. Each day I wonder how much longer this will last. But I know that it can't go on much longer. You ask in today's letter about moving to yourself. Darling, I am sure you would be making a mistake as Mom and Pop are so much help with the children. I so admire you for trying to save like you do, but, darling, don't move yet. It won't be another summer pass by before I am home. And I must remember that I am out here where I don't have the slightest ideas what prices are or even the value of money any more. Darling Polly wouldn't understand so much, so tell her Daddy is always thinking of her wishes so much he could see her. I know I am fighting for a better life for us and surely we shall be granted that. Remember every minute that I love you truly and I know you love me with all your heart. Goodnight for tonight, darling, and tell my boy and girl goodnight.

Well, that's all for now. Except that Pat and Sue's mule Katy got out of the pasture yesterday and was trotting across the highway to go visit at Turley's station when she was rudely approached by a red Ford Escort on its way to Marshall. The Ford Escort left strips of tire for yards and yards down the highway and managed to almost come to a stop. It tapped Katy a little tap on the behind, and Katy jumped the car *endways*. There are eyewitnesses to this. As Katy was coming down, she gave one of those mule snap-kicks and did $935 worth of damage to the rear end of the car. She then trotted home to Pat and Sue's. The people in the car followed. So did the eyewitnesses. Sue came to the back door and looked out, saw Katy, saw the enraged people, saw the eyewitnesses, saw the bashed-in Ford Escort, and cried out, "Pat!! Pat!! There's a *strange mule* in our backyard!"

This forest fire was splendid, it was prodigal; Fire #33 burning up 3,456 acres or something like that. They took me up in a two-passenger helicopter. My partner The Shooter says helicopters have a godlike aspect in that they levitate and ascend vertically when they leave the earth and also that they throw up such a roar and a large amount of debris that people bend down and avert their faces. There were three, four big ones levitating and ascending from the fire base. They were bucket-bombing the hot spots. The pilot took off the door so I could hang out and shoot pictures, and I saw what an appreciable amount of air was between me and the ground. The pilot doesn't give a shit if you fall out. He just wants to whizz us around the fire and then get back to bucket-bombing. I don't think they're into flying picture-taking people around. We were about two hundred feet over this enormous spruce that torched; that's what the fire fighters say. They say "torch." It was on the edge of the hottest part of the burn and I guess it was surrounded by so much pure-D temperature that it went incandescent in seconds. The fire shot up it and it burst; it started burning sideways like an explosion. We had headsets with mikes so everybody could talk to each other because the chopper was making movie-sound-track chopper sounds. I heard the pilot say, "God, I can't wait to get rid of these shooters and get back to bucket-bombing." Then we landed in some muskeg because I wanted a shot of the ground crew and they did it: they all fell to their knees in attitudes of devotion and put their hard hats over their faces as we came down. That's the other thing; because of the rotor-drop, you have to grovel and sort of crawl up to the helicopter when you board it, and do the same thing in reverse as you leave The Presence. The really big ones come down among the crews at the fire base and there are all these groveling fire fighters with chips and shit and dust and bits of gravel flying. These guys go at fire fighting as if it were a military operation. They speak of the "initial attack" and fires that "resist attack." Vietnam has done a lot of weird things to the world. The Chinese are over here studying with the Northern Ontario Ministry of Natural Resources because the Ontario MNR are the best fire fighters in the world and they will tell you so. So while we were hovering and levitating over the torching spruce, it hit me that this is what Moses saw. One is in The Presence of The Flame. Different kinds of energy take place in different parts of the world. Up here it's fire. There have always been fires up here. That's how the boreal forest remakes itself: the spruce cones can't open up and generate seeds until they've been through a forest fire. They're too hard, they have to be burnt open. That's how it works. Maybe that's how we work. I came away with the conviction that if you consistently search for synchronized moments in the hottest places of your heart, you will get what you look for; and the Cosmic Helicopter Pilot will say:

Watch this!

Watch this happen!

It's a matter of getting your eye behind it and focusing, and to just keep on watching and not freak or fall out.

And so this is the fire season happening up here in Sioux Lookout.

A NOTE ABOUT THE AUTHOR

Paulette Jiles was born in Missouri, in the Ozarks, in 1943, where she grew up in the town of Blackwater. She moved to Canada in 1969. For some years she worked in the Arctic as a journalist and news photographer. Her book of poems Celestial Navigation *won the 1984 Governor General's Literary Award, making Jiles the first American to receive the prize for a work of poetry.* Celestial Navigation *was also honored with the Gerald Lampert Memorial Award and the Pat Lowther Award. Jiles has brought out two other volumes of poetry,* Waterloo Express, *a collection, and* The James Poems, *a cycle of poems turning on the activities of the Jesse James gang. She is also the author of a prose-poem novella,* A Manual of Etiquette for Ladies Crossing Canada by Train.

A NOTE ON THE TYPE

The text of this book was set in a digitized version of Fairfield, a typeface designed by the distinguished American artist and engraver Rudolph Ruzicka (1883–1978). Fairfield displays the sober and sane qualities of a master craftsman whose talent has long been dedicated to clarity. Rudolph Ruzicka was born in Bohemia and came to America in 1894. He designed and illustrated many books and was the creator of a considerable list of individual prints in a variety of techniques.

Composed by Brevis Press, Bethany, Connecticut. Printed and bound by R. R. Donnelley & Sons, Harrisonburg, Virginia.

Designed by Iris Weinstein.